effective
college
teaching

THE CONTRIBUTORS

Joseph Axelrod
Kenneth B. Boulding
Stanford C. Ericksen
Garrett Hardin
O. B. Hardison, Jr.
Harold Hodgkinson
Robert B. MacLeod
Lewis Mayhew
Morris H. Shamos
R. L. Wilder

effective college teaching

THE QUEST FOR RELEVANCE

William H. Morris, *Editor*

Published for American Association for Higher Education
by American Council on Education

SBN 8268-1273-2
Library of Congress Catalog Card Number 73-113878

The work presented herein was performed pursuant to a contract
with the U.S. Office of Education HEW. However, the opinions
expressed herein do not necessarily reflect the position of the U.S.
Office of Education and no official endorsement should be inferred.

Contents

Preface   vii

Introduction: The College Teacher Today   xi
     RUSSELL COOPER

Earning and Learning by the Hour   1
     STANFORD C. ERICKSEN

Teaching Styles in the Humanities   38
     JOSEPH AXELROD

Teaching the Humanities   56
     O. B. HARDISON, JR.

The Art of Teaching Science   66
     MORRIS H. SHAMOS

A Path to Relevant Teaching   87
     GARRETT HARDIN

The Beginning Teacher
of College Mathematics   94
     R. L. WILDER

The Task of the Teacher
in the Social Sciences   104
     KENNETH B. BOULDING

The Teaching of Psychology   124
     ROBERT B. MACLEOD

The Organization of the Profession   133
     LEWIS MAYHEW

Finding the Levers   148
     HAROLD HODGKINSON

Appendix: Bibliographies
for Additional Fields   159

Preface

"Teaching assistants all too often become flunkies and not teaching assistants at all. It is almost a misnomer." The speaker was one of a group of new college teachers in the biological sciences brought together to discuss the preservice preparation of teachers as they had experienced it. Most had been teaching for a year or so, but some were graduate students in the process of gaining their degrees. Most, but not all, of those present had held teaching assistantships.

According to several of the young teachers, the preparation did not anticipate demands of the job in the areas of lecture preparation, setting up labs, faculty committee work, student advising, developing a philosophy of teaching, and giving courses outside their own fields of concentration. It is surely not surprising that some graduate schools had been more effective than others, in the opinion of the recipients, in offering a broad and effective preparation.[1]

Speaking to the same group, Lyle W. Phillips, director, Undergraduate Education in Science, National Science Foundation, put it succinctly: "I have the feeling that a straight Ph.D. course in biology that gives the student no opportunity to think or to learn a little bit about the teaching and learning process is not the kind of program that is going to produce the best kind of college teacher."

It is sometimes said of college teaching that, while there is an apprenticeship of sorts, it is the only profession that does not uniformly require formal preparation for admission into its ranks. If this assertion is accepted as valid for past practice, then the trends of recent years have contributed little to stabilizing the pattern of induction. Consider a few trends that have emerged: (1) the surge in total college enrollment, (2) the growth of two-year institutions, (3) the increase in the number of teaching assistantships, (4) the acceleration in the growth of knowledge and particularly in ways of organizing it, (5) the rise of vocal discontent with the curricular offerings and the resultant cry for the reexamination of the whole college program. That which has always been surrounded with a certain mystique—induction into the profession —is now exposed to new and complex problems.

No one volume, probably not even a collection of volumes, can make up for lacunae in preparation or bring about the creation of the nearly perfect teacher. It is hoped, however, that the present small book may contribute, along with other works in the literature, to serving some of the needs expressed by the teachers newly entered into college work.

This book is a selection of chapters from a larger collection prepared

---

1. The full report is available from the Commission on Undergraduate Education in the Biological Sciences (Washington, D. C.) Memo no. 69-18, Nov. 4, 1969.

as a study of college teaching with special reference to the disciplines. The study was conducted under contract with the U.S. Office of Education and under the auspices of the Joint Committee on College Teaching (JCOT) for which the American Association for Higher Education serves as administrative and fiscal agent. The present volume is a direct descendant of the earlier study completed in 1969 with the inverted title, *The Quest for Relevance: Effective College Teaching*. The JCOT, as sponsor of that study, was responding to a widespread concern about the quality of college teaching. While it must not be assumed that each association endorses all parts of the work, the JCOT has included representatives of the USOE and of the following professional associations:

> American Association for the Advancement of Science
> American Association for Higher Education
> American Association of Junior Colleges
> American Chemical Society
> American Council on Education
> American Council of Learned Societies
> American Economic Association
> American Historical Association
> American Institute of Biological Sciences
> American Institute of Physics
> American Political Science Association
> American Psychological Association
> College English Association
> Conference Board of the Mathematical Sciences
> Modern Language Association of America

It is a cardinal fact of academic life that teachers primarily identify themselves with disciplines and become members of professional associations based on the disciplines. In delineating the nature of the study, however, the JCOT found itself driven toward a discernible interdisciplinary stance. Joseph Axelrod's "teaching styles in the humanities" can find exponents in all fields. Kenneth Boulding's nine "queries" hardly apply only to a teacher in economics, or even in the social sciences. Morris Shamos speaks of the techniques of teaching science, not physics or chemistry. Similarly, those writing from the vantage of a particular discipline were encouraged not to feel constricted in their own fields; most were not. Further, each of the contributors was asked to examine the current trends in teaching in his discipline or area and to evaluate them.

In effect, the JCOT says that the road to more effective college teaching lies not in turning away from scholarship but in learning simultaneously more about other disciplines, the principles of teaching, and the complex institutions that universities have become. To be a whole teacher, one's active awareness must spread beyond scholarship in his own specialty, and beyond teaching in his own field. Viewed this way, the sharpened focus that comes with concentration on the fewer disciplines represented in this volume as compared with the original study may be highly salutary. A new teacher in any field—if he aspires to more than mere craftsmanship—will, it is hoped, gain as much from all parts of the book as from a treatment of his own discipline.

It hardly seems sufficient merely to list the members of the Advisory Committee, drawn largely from the JCOT itself. Both individually and collectively they gave shape and point to the original study. By consensus of the contributors, the text was also greatly strengthened by the editorial ministrations of Ada Jane Kelly.

ADVISORY COMMITTEE

Russell M. Cooper, University of South Florida, chairman
Bruce Dearing, State University of New York at Binghampton
Maxwell H. Goldberg, Pennsylvania State University
Harold L. Hodgkinson, University of California, Berkeley
Arthur H. Livermore, American Association for the Advancement of Science
Paul L. Ward, American Historical Association
Winslow R. Hatch, Division of Higher Education Research, U.S. Office of Education
Robert G. Bone, Illinois State University, project director

WILLIAM H. MORRIS
Associate Executive
American Association for Higher Education

Introduction
The College Teacher Today

RUSSELL COOPER

I will do such things, —
What they are, yet I know not; but they shall be
The terrors of the earth!
KING LEAR

At a time when inarticulate fury and a deep sense of betrayal are being translated into irrational violence on American campuses, it behooves the teaching profession to consider seriously the inadequacies and lapses of which it stands accused. Under the best of circumstances, teachers should be eager and active in searching out ways to improve their performance. Now, more than ever before, the public at large and the young in particular pose penetrating questions for institutions of higher learning. Teachers are called upon to defend the relevance of the subject matter they offer, to adopt new styles and techniques in teaching an ever-increasing number of students with varying backgrounds and disparate expectations, and to consider the influence, actual and potential, of higher education upon the social problems of the day.

In the quieter past the home, the church, and to a degree industry have been dominant influences on the culture and mores of the nation. Now institutions of higher learning find themselves closer to the center of the stage than ever before. An inescapable by-product of this new eminence and influence is responsibility for ensuring relevance in subject matter, for giving challenge and intellectual excitement in provision and guidance of learning experiences and for enlightening leadership in the development and improvement of society.

Ironically, at the very time when all components of society are demanding both greater educational opportunity and college graduates with increased competence—willing and able to bring new order, justice, and human dignity to a world in chaos—much that the university has traditionally offered is scorned and rejected. At the very time the conscientious teacher is striving to present relevant concepts, information, and techniques effectively to rapidly multiplying numbers of

Dr. Cooper is dean, College of Liberal Arts, University of South Florida, and chairman, Joint Committee on College Teaching.

impatient students, he must face vast amounts of new knowledge which should be sorted, assimilated, reorganized, and prepared for the classroom.

This volume has been written in the conviction that, while most teachers are well aware of the difficulties and satisfactions of effective teaching and share the assumption that there is no single exclusive method of excellent teaching, both the novice instructor and the senior professor can profit from a fresh and direct examination of the process of teaching and learning in higher education. Most academics concede that there is no such person as a "perfect" teacher and that any teacher who is genuinely content with his performance merely demonstrates that his goals were so modest it was possible for him to reach them. No responsible teacher lays claim to final truths which will guarantee perfection in the practice of teaching; nevertheless, many young teachers can learn much from those who have continued to learn and have been willing to test new ideas and to adapt those that proved successful. Veteran teachers can offer reliable suggestions concerning ventures likely to be productive and those likely to continue to lead to frustration and failure.

Students know—and act upon their knowledge—that some teachers are more effective than others, not merely or even necessarily more learned, but more resourceful in engaging and exciting students and launching them on intellectual adventures of their own. Students also often recognize more astutely than faculty colleagues or academic administrators that many teachers are at their best with particular kinds of students but with other types either fail to challenge or to be appropriately compassionate. The lackluster lecturer may be a deft and probing seminar leader; the brilliant and dramatic expositor may be the overbearing monologist who frustrates small-group discussion. Whatever his gifts or limitations, the teacher with a vocation must be alertly self-critical; he must seek continually for increased effectiveness in communication and intellectual engagement; he must check repeatedly and with painful honesty to ensure that the knowledge he endeavors to communicate and the skills he seeks to develop are, and are demonstrated to be, relevant to the time and to the students.

This work has been designed primarily for those newly embarked upon a teaching career, whether as neophyte faculty members at the end of graduate preparation or as teaching assistants in a university. But even the veteran teacher, like the admirable Clerk of Oxenford, with a mind open to fresh suggestion should find much in these pages to inspire reflection and experimentation. Individual readers may be more interested in some chapters than in others; however, a reading of the whole book should repay the effort, as it sets the task of teaching in full perspective.

This work reflects a deep and abiding common concern among leaders of national professional societies for the improvement of quality and the insurance of relevance in teaching in their fields. If it succeeds in stimulating teachers to improve the practice of their art and craft and if it sustains them in their efforts, all those who have contributed to it will be richly rewarded.

Earning and Learning by the Hour

STANFORD C. ERICKSEN

In the golden age of teaching—before printing, electricity, and grade-point ratios—the role of the teacher was to conserve and transmit knowledge and to inspire students to inquire into themselves and the world around them. Despite the technological and social complexities that entangle higher education today, these purposes remain. The practical problem is implementation: how can the instructor best utilize the available resources to direct the academic progress of students? This chapter, therefore, deals with practical matters of instruction, with the means by which the teacher and the student can best achieve their ends in the classroom.

PEDAGOGICAL IMPRINTING

First impressions are important. Every new instructor knows this from his own experience as a student. Having been for many years a spectator to the teaching process, he has witnessed firsthand the many different ways of teaching and has favored some over others. It is through this process, more than through formal teacher-training procedures, that his own image of good teaching most likely took form. Preparation for college teaching usually emphasizes substantive knowledge almost to the exclusion of the practical aspects of teaching. When the graduate student moves to the other side of the desk to practice, without much practice, what he has observed for so long, he is understandably concerned about his competence as a classroom teacher.

In response to his inquiries, or perhaps as a matter of form, a department chairman, dean, or senior professor might advise the beginning teacher of the departmental and institutional traditions and conventions for classroom conduct and administrative obligation. These briefings may include admonishments ranging from rules on smoking to matters of in loco parentis. The decision on how many of these an instructor will accept, ignore, shade, conform to, or perhaps extend will be made and remade throughout his career.

At any rate, on the first day of class career plans become reality.

Dr. Ericksen is director, Center for Research on Learning and Teaching, University of Michigan.

1

The exciting mix of anticipation and anxiety in meeting a class for the first time is not restricted to the rookie; even an old pro often senses a dry mouth and sweating palms when he walks into the classroom for the first meeting of the term. Teachers particularly sensitive about personal relations with students may start out by giving considerable attention to matters of class procedure and to their own and students' responsibilities. Those with a stronger content orientation may use this first hour to outline the curricular substance of the course and to proceed immediately with the initial lecture.

Whether the emphasis is on procedure or content, the anxious teacher should avoid untried flamboyancies, stage tricks, and other contrived attempts to impress students. It is extremely difficult to play an artificial role over a full semester of exposure to and critical observation by an intelligent audience. On the first day, or on any other day, a teacher is in no position to deviate from the consistency of his natural manner of talking, thinking, and behaving.

The teacher's initial responsibility is to define clearly his instructional objectives. He need not necessarily do this on the first day of class, although he might make a start on the means of achieving content objectives by describing the taxonomies that will be used, the nature of assignments, and the conduct of examinations, including the ground rules for grading and evaluation.

Generalizations about what, when, and how a teacher does things nearly always have to be reinterpreted to meet the instructional specifics of a given content area, the particular habits and traits of each teacher, and the differing backgrounds, abilities, and expectations of students. Teaching freshmen in a two-year community college, for example, is quite different from teaching seniors in a large university. Advanced students have learned how to be college students; they know the tactics and strategies for the care and feeding of teachers, and they realize the varying weights to be assigned the different competitive elements among students and between students and teachers— the games these people play.

Even so, and despite the differences between teachers, departments, and schools, most students start a course with certain common questions. On the first day of class they seek answers to four questions.

1. Does the teacher care?

Most teachers and students prefer small classes for the good reason that in small groups they can relate to one another and be recognized as distinct and real persons rather than as seat numbers to be evaluated by an electronic test-scoring machine. An instructor who does not enjoy teaching and who has no particular interest in his class as individuals will very likely not be well received by the students. If he does not care, neither do the students, regardless of his teaching style. The same effect is generated by those professors whose primary interest is research rather than teaching and who look on their classes as forced obligations. They hope students will not bother them and will leave them free to pursue the library or laboratory projects that are presumed to bring higher status.

If in succeeding class meetings the instructor gives valid evidence that he is trying to communicate with students, that he does care sincerely about their progress, that he makes whatever adaptations are possible to meet the individual interests and abilities of his students, quite likely they will accept him and endorse his teaching. The teacher who likes his students and who enjoys teaching has what most certainly must be universal characteristics of successful teaching.

2. Is the teacher fair?

Students are more likely to object to unfair treatment than to excessive demands in assignments and work load. As long as they feel that the competition is fair, individual students will proceed to achieve at the level consistent with their interests and abilities and prerequisite qualifications. Students also judge the fairness of the teacher by his classroom manner; a teacher's pet is no less an irritant to college students than he is to elementary-school pupils.

3. Does the teacher know the subject matter?

Students are not uncritical judges of an instructor's subject-matter competence. Experienced teachers develop various techniques for buffering, bluffing, or bamboozling critical students on topics about which they feel insecure, ignorant, or indifferent. When these techniques are appropriate, if they ever are, is a matter for individual judgment. It is doubtful, however, that incompetence in subject matter can long be covered up in meeting the minimal requirements for effective college teaching.

4. How is the course relevant?

Is the course relevant to me, the student might wonder, or to the problems of the world around me—or mainly to the subject-matter specialist? Students have pressed the word *relevance* to the point of diminishing returns. Despite linguistic distractions, relevance and similar concepts—validity, usefulness, utility, generality, application —remain significant factors against which students and faculty will evaluate a particular course of instruction. Since relevance implies a value judgment, the instructor must differentiate the source of this appraisal; if a topic is relevant to the student's further understanding of the parent discipline, it should not be compromised in response to demands from the students who are looking only for the applications of a given body of knowledge to a contemporary social problem.

Nevertheless, and in contrast to an earlier day, fewer and fewer college courses can be defended primarily on the basis of their intrinsic worth and without reference to the value of the course content (broadly defined) to external problems and issues.

Sometime during his first term of teaching, the new instructor might well seek the advice and counsel of an experienced teacher. Institutions vary widely in this practice,[1] but whether voluntary or imposed, supervision is often considered by the apprentice teacher to be the single most needed provision in his preparation as a teacher.

This chapter is one step in a practical exercise in the application of theory; the concepts are here, but their application remains the responsibility of the individual instructor. College teachers are quite capable of interpreting and utilizing for their own purposes the factual statements, propositions, and value judgments here presented concerning their three most important responsibilities: student motivation, learning, and evaluation.

GENERATING AND MAINTAINING STUDENT INTEREST

The art of teaching is in no way better exemplified than in the ability of a teacher to increase a student's motivation to learn. Even so, college teachers do not, for the most part, make a public display of the talent to inspire, particularly not in the presence of colleagues. The older academic culture views teachers and students as rational men seeking "truth without consequences"[2] and discipline purity without mission utility. For a long time, therefore, motivating students to learn has been part of the hidden agenda of teaching.

Yet, teaching is not a form of psychotherapy, and the teacher should be less concerned with personality dynamics in general than with the dynamics of learning and thinking. As vital as motivation is, it should not be separated from the content of a course. The teacher motivates by precept and by example, not by showmanship, and in this way gives evidence that the material in his course is worth learning.

Until recently, the purpose of higher education was mental discipline and character building, and motivation was thought to be best controlled through punishment and the threat of punishment. Today higher education states its goals explicitly in terms of the content students learn and the attitudes they acquire; therein lies its educational relevance and, therefore, its appeal. Teachers and students alike want to locate and make use of the conditions that determine how

1. Frank Koen, "The Training of Graduate Student Teaching Assistants."
2. Carl Schorske, quoted in Malcolm G. Scully, "Academic Turmoil Grows over Moves to 'Politicize' Universities, Associations."

much and how well subject matter is learned. Thus, the practical relationship between teaching and motivation is about the same as the theoretical relationship between learning and motivation, an interaction that has been thoroughly described in the research literature.

It is generally agreed that motivation is an extremely powerful, if not a necessary, factor in the learning process. A student's motivational level changes significantly during a one-semester lecture course, for example. Most of the time he loafs along; then the next examination is announced and he moves into action. As the hour of the test approaches, his level of anxiety may actually exceed the optimum level of motivation for effective learning. Bruner has an interesting observation on this point:

> Somewhere between apathy and wild excitement, there is an optimum level of aroused attention that is ideal for classroom activity. What is that level? Frenzied activity fostered by the competitive project may leave no pause for reflection, for evaluation, for generalization, while excessive orderliness, with each student waiting passively for his turn, produces boredom and ultimate apathy. There is a day-to-day problem here of great significance. Short-run arousal of interest is not the same as the long-term establishment of interest in the broader sense. . . . The issue is particularly relevant in an entertainment-oriented, mass-communication culture where passivity and "spectatorship" are dangers. Perhaps it is in the technique of arousing attention in school that first steps can be taken to establish that active autonomy of attention that is the antithesis of the spectator's passivity.[3]

The motivational complexities of a college class can be seen (inferred) among students taking a required course. The student who enters a core course with a positive attitude and genuine desire to acquire a particular body of knowledge represents quite a different motivational set (expectation) from the set of a student who is critical and suspicious or has a negative or resentful attitude toward the requirement. Students with sharply differing motivational sets do not hear or read the same things and to a certain extent may hardly be participating in the same course. Fortunately, most students are able to mask rather specific negative sets for a given course by their stronger interests in maintaining self-esteem, achieving their levels of academic aspiration, and appearing to be congenial and contributing members of a group.

3. Jerome S. Bruner, *The Process of Education*, p. 72.

EXTRINSIC MOTIVATION

A maxim of learning theory states that reward is more powerful than
punishment in changing behavior. Psychologists did not discover the
phenomenon of reinforcement; they simply took an age-old principle
of behavior into the laboratory in an attempt to describe more specifically the relationship between reward, punishment, and behavior
change. The task of the teacher, however, is to provide in a natural,
sensible, honest, and forthright way the reinforcing information and
events for the student.

Fear and punishment. Despite its well-established place in education, punishment remains the enemy of good instruction. The protection and support given punitive methods by the educational system
and its traditions notwithstanding, this negative method of control is
essentially a lazy man's way of teaching, and the consequence is too
often a widening breach in the personal relations between the teacher
and the student. Skinner has analyzed the educational effects of
punishment:

> Whether maintained by the physical environment, the social
> environment, or the teacher, punishing contingencies are no
> doubt effective, but their mode of operation is easily misun-
> derstood. Where positive reinforcement builds up behavior,
> negative reinforcement seems to break it down, but the effect
> is not quite so simple. . . . By punishing behavior we wish to
> suppress, we arrange conditions under which acceptable be-
> havior is strengthened, but the contingencies do not specify
> the form of the latter behavior. When we punish a student who
> displeases us, we do not specify pleasing behavior. The student
> learns only indirectly to avoid or escape our punishment, pos-
> sibly by acquiring some of the techniques of self-management.[4]

The variety and the range of reinforcing contingencies are considerable, but many are not particularly related to achievement of the
objectives of a specific instructional program. Pleasing the teacher,
staying eligible, earning a scholarship and special awards, or getting
a better job by virtue of a high grade-average are all motives that are
extrinsic to the subject matter itself and are of questionable reward
value. Nevertheless, they are there, and to many students they are
the controlling reasons for study and academic achievement.

Grades. The course grade is one of the most powerful incentives at
the teacher's disposal. Earning a high grade serves strong and varied
motives. Whatever the skill or knowledge of the teacher, whatever his

4. B. F. Skinner, *The Technology of Teaching,* p. 186.

discipline or method of instruction, the anticipation of being graded will influence the student to learn material he expects to be asked about on an examination. McKeachie suggests that the failure to establish the superiority of one teaching method over another may be in part because motivation to earn grades per se is so strong that it overrides the effects of most teaching methods.[5]

Attention is selective, and students tend to structure material they read and hear around their expectations about the kind of examination they will confront. If they expect to be asked for unassimilated facts, they will memorize; if they expect to be required to integrate, extend, and evaluate, they will work toward those ends. To utilize fully the incentive value of grades, the teacher must ask: Will a high score on this examination indicate that the student has met the instructional objectives I have set for this course? If not, the teacher has neglected a powerful and relevant incentive.

In an early study it was found that, given ten reasons for wanting to earn good grades, students said the most important was to receive a good "recommendation for a job" and second, "to indicate that I am actually learning something: new facts, how to think, etc." The relative weights given the various reasons differed markedly from one group of students to another, indicating the complex and distinctive pattern of motives of individual students.[6] Recognition of these differences should supplement the instructor's understanding of individual student's abilities and aptitudes.

INTRINSIC MOTIVATION

The ability to relate subject matter with the student's own aspirations and values is probably one of the defining characteristics of the master teacher. By the time a serious student comes to college, he has developed a strong curiosity, a continuing interest in searching for concepts and principles that will integrate and give meaning to otherwise diverse events. Conceptual ordering can be exciting and most likely becomes so when a student has the intellectual freedom to seek the information that will reduce his own uncertainties.

Reward without grades. The subjective feeling of understanding can be its own reward; McKee found that a well-programmed unit on basic electronics held the interest of a group of young adults in a correctional institution who, probably for the first time in their lives, were participating in an intrinsically rewarding educational experience. Fader and Schaevitz's delightful report *Hooked on Books* recon-

5. Wilbert J. McKeachie, "Motivation, Teaching Methods, and College Learning."

6. Stanford C. Ericksen, "An Experimental Study of Individual Differences in Scholastic Motives," p. 510.

firms the power of self-directed achievement to promote academic progress among "poor learners." It describes a training school program in which boys were encouraged to read or write about whatever they wanted and were rewarded for their gross accomplishment rather than punished for what they had not read or not said correctly. The most dramatic example of success is a boy, essentially illiterate when the program began, who later published a book of poetry.[7]

The college teacher today and in the forseeable future must learn to utilize intrinsic motivation and to restructure his subject matter and instructional procedures so that his course becomes relevant, either to a larger aspect of the discipline or to some aspects of society, or both. The first teach-in (1964) at the University of Michigan, for example, was an intense educational experience for students and faculty alike. It had nothing to do with grades, but in the eyes of those attending, it had everything to do with the relevance of higher education to an important issue in society at large.

How far the teacher can go in adapting his course to the personal interests and needs of each student, in addition to the needs of society and of his discipline, depends partly on the size of his class and on his own abilities and his interests in bringing about these individualized adaptations. The final responsibility must rest with the student, however, since he can best match his own intellectual curiosities with the corresponding elements in the course itself. For example, he can write his term paper or conduct a special project on those topics that interest him most and have greater relevance to his personal program of education and his career aspirations.

Intellectual curiosity. Intellectual curiosity is the best single example of intrinsic motivation in education.

> To those who agree with Samuel Johnson that "Curiosity is in great and generous minds the first passion and the last," the motive that impels the quest for knowledge for its own sake is inestimably more important than the various kinds of extrinsic motives directed toward the attainment of grades. If classroom incentives for learning have been nothing more than the extrinsic satisfactions to which good grades are instrumental, what will remain when the last exam is turned in and the threat or promise of a course grade no longer looms to control and direct learning? If, on the other hand, learning in college has been intrinsically satisfying, and if curiosity has been fostered, is it not more likely that questioning and searching will continue throughout a lifetime?[8]

7. John M. McKee, "The Draper Experiment"; Daniel N. Fader and Morton H. Schaevitz, *Hooked on Books.*
8. Patricia O'Connor, "Motivation to Learn," p. 20.

Just as he cannot deal squarely with most of the other important incentives for learning, the teacher cannot appeal directly to students' intellectual curiosity. Understanding and meaning speak for themselves, and if the organization and sequencing of a course are well done and if the teacher can arrange conditions so that a student can evaluate his own progress, the teacher's "problem" of student motivation to learn will almost take care of itself. The student can pace himself at the rate and in qualitative patterns that are most compatible with the curiosity that brought him into the course; he will learn what he needs to know to reduce the uncertainty and to resolve the cognitive conflicts and the confusion and complexities, the ambiguities that form, in sum, the ideal profile of academic motivation.

SOCIAL SUPPORT

Students of this generation and those in the forseeable future will acquire strong people-linked habits of learning. Understanding the motivation that a student brings to class requires that the teacher take into account the larger academic atmosphere within which the student studies, works, and plays. As Feldman and Newcomb, Astin, Brown, Sanford, and many others have shown, the outside-of-class experiences of students with their families, their peers, the faculty, and the community are dominant influences in shaping academic plans and aspirations.[9] From infancy most of what a child learns is directly conditioned to other people; from that point on the child is constantly being "educated," rewarded and punished, as he moves along one learning curve after another within an environment of other people. Students are not students per se, that is, logical and rational learners; they are young adults with feelings, ambitions, and anxieties and with sensitivity to and concern about their relations with others. Communication between teacher and student requires an appreciation of these dynamic social and personal factors so important in shaping the academic achievement of students.

The residence hall. The long-term effects of a college education—especially the attitudes, the values, and the interests carried away by the graduate—are more likely the consequence of experiences outside the classroom than the result of formal classroom instruction. The movement among large universities to establish residential colleges can be justified and defended on many grounds, but high priority should be given to the role the residential experience can play in generally coalescing educational aspirations and, more particularly, in reinforcing motivation to learn.

9. Kenneth A. Feldman and Theodore M. Newcomb, *The Impacts of College on Students;* A. W. Astin, *The College Environment;* Donald R. Brown, "Student Stress and the Institutional Environment"; Nevitt Sanford, *Where Colleges Fail.*

By assigning roommates and some floormates who also are class-mates and by providing easy access to resident teaching fellows and to senior faculty, a well-planned residential program in a large uni-versity can recover a great deal of the academic and social interplay that characterizes the small liberal arts college.[10] Discontinuity be-tween formal classroom work and extracurricular activities seriously reduces the motivational support for academic achievement. An ideal residential college overcomes the rupture between the student's aca-demic work and his personal and social activities outside the classroom.

The home. Most college students in the United States live at home, but even those who are "away at college" carry with them the influence of their families. Numerous studies, especially those of Thistle-thwaite, Astin, and Holland, have found that the educational aspira-tions a student brings with him—for example, to earn a Ph.D. or an M.D.—have a greater influence on his achievement than has the separate or added influence of his undergraduate college. According to these studies, the fact that such a large proportion of graduates from select liberal arts colleges seek advanced degrees is more a function of the kinds of students who go to such colleges than of the institutional effect itself.[11] These are not, of course, hard and fast distinctions, and the value of this research rests primarily on underlining the lasting motivational effects of the home and the home community.

Extracurricular activities. To most teachers on the wrong side of the generation gap, the phrase *extracurricular activities* means such playtime involvements as athletics, dances, publications, and fraternity life. These still exist, but their influence may be progressively declin-ing as students become more involved in social change in the com-munity at large. For example, undergraduates and faculty at a number of institutions have been meeting out of common interest to arrange courses of study oriented almost entirely around the social, political, economic, educational, and other problems presented by ghetto life in contemporary America. The dichotomy between curricu-lar and extracurricular pursuits is becoming less distinct as the student protest for greater educational relevance becomes louder and more fre-quent. The changing extracurricular activities of students are a reminder of their educational interests. Homecoming queens are still nice to look at, but they are rapidly becoming symbols of a college purpose that is drifting by as students themselves are reordering their priorities.

10. Ellis Wunsch, "The Pilot Project."
11. D. L. Thistlethwaite, "College Press and Changes in Study Plans of Talented Students"; A. W. Astin, "Undergraduate Institutions and the Production of Scien-tists"; J. L. Holland, "Determinants of College Choice."

PERSONAL GOALS

A predictive test of a student's level of motivation, if one existed, would undoubtedly be as valid as prevailing correlations with verbal and mathematical aptitude tests. Teachers recognize that some students are simply more ambitious than others and have a stronger drive to achieve, to succeed, and to excel. The characteristic motive of a second group of students can be described in terms of anxieties and fear of failure, while a third might show a greater need for affiliation, for friendship, for personal support, affection, and the like. Actually, of course, each of us, teachers and students alike, can be plotted at the intersect of an almost infinite array of characteristics. As tempting and as convenient as it might be, the teacher must avoid accepting a neat pigeonhole classification of student motivation and focus his attention more sharply on the educational interests of each student as an autonomous, independent, and unique person.

Level of aspiration. Most students are quite self-critical and sensitive about their levels of performance. Considerable research has been directed at the relation between the student's expectation when he starts the task—or course—and the level of his final performance. Empirical studies show that rewarding achievements beyond a preset level will produce greater change in behavior than will punishing failure to achieve the expected level of performance. The teacher should, therefore, be more concerned with lowering the level of aspiration for slow or weak students than with raising the level of aspiration for those who aim too low.

Unfortunately, a student's level of aspiration is too often linked with grades and the quality-point ratio. Instructors can help a student reshape his ambitions toward specific academic achievement by making qualitative evaluations of reports, papers, performance on examinations, and the like. This type of personal recognition does the student a marked educational service by helping him to discriminate between grades as housekeeping or management devices and intellectual achievement as the proper end of education.

Interests, attitudes, and values. The conforming student is easy to teach, but the uncritical acceptance of chunks of knowledge does not add up to the kind of complete education needed to cope successfully with the wild rush of scientific and technological change and to understand social conflicts and issues. It is the constellation of interests, attitudes, and values the subject matter can help to formulate that will remain with students long after factual information and concept labels are forgotten or found to be obsolete or irrelevant. The instructor must therefore accept the further responsibility of defining attitudes and values that he believes to be appropriate goals of his course. However, the line between instruction and indoctrination is sometimes indistinct, and unless attitude changes and values are explicitly defined early in the course, the instructor may be vulnerable to charges of brainwashing and thought control.

Interests, attitudes, and values are all motivational in their behavioral effects. It follows, therefore, that a central task of the teacher—one that cannot be transferred to the computer or to the counselor—will be to direct the learning and thinking of each student along lines that are consistent and compatible with the motivational profile he brings to class. Motives carry the important function of screening either in or out the kind of ideas that the student incorporates into his thinking, his aspirations, and his actions.

Student discontent. Student discontent over specific courses and specific teachers is old hat. The new phenomenon is discontent with the institution—for example, with residential life, with student participation in university decision making, or with the official role of the university in community and national affairs. These protests extend beyond the specific adaptations that a given teacher might make for a given course. Nevertheless, a significant change is taking place: the teacher is coming under growing pressure to become involved with value judgments. He is being urged to go beyond the traditional information-giving function to help students define their base-line humane values as they relate to society and to the current and future developments of the discipline. The instructor is in a position to help students combine means with ends, to link methodology with content, and to validate both in terms of the social purposes of higher education.

Love and other miscellaneous motives. Sex seems to interest college students (and others), but whether sex is related to learning and thinking is a matter for which data are elusive. Nevertheless, the new instructor soon becomes aware that the classroom is a game preserve for activities that are tangential or parallel or orthogonal to the educational purpose of the course. Any discussion of student motivation must, therefore, at least recognize the *miscellaneous* category. The instructor considers education as studying and going to class, but many students, unfortunately, view these hallmarks simply as indirect means of fulfilling personal interests. A request from a student to his teacher may be important to one but trivial, if not out of order, to the other.

The solution, theoretical or practical, to this underlying conflict of interests is hard to come by. Rather than launch a counterattack, the teacher might find some way to justify an instructional "time-out."

The announcement, for example, that an important examination will be given on the last class meeting before or on the day after a holiday or a significant personal event might demonstrate the pervasive authority of the instructor, but it will not substantially promote the academic excellence of the student. Equally unproductive may be the opposite extreme—an overly permissive class in which the content, the rate of progress, and the evaluation procedures are mainly under the control of the students, with the instructor being simply a passive logistical agent. Permissiveness has its place, but not as an alternative to the instructor's definition of course objectives and his active role in arranging conditions for the achievement of these goals by his students. To bend to every whim of the students and to seek aggressively an informal atmosphere—All you students can call me Joe— too often tells the students: I am more anxious that you like me than that you learn something.

Learning, Thinking, and Attitude Change

The mystique of teaching serves as a buffer between the teacher and many of the outside criteria that might be used to evaluate his contribution to the learning process. The topics and the point of view in this section give only passing attention to developing teaching style in favor of defining a view of the college teacher as the person responsible for setting the goals of a course of study and controlling the means by which these goals are achieved.

LEARNING THEORY AND TEACHING

Learning theory is the best source for the logic and the meaning behind the instructional process. Principles of learning provide a stabilizing foundation in those places where the educational sands are shifting. Unfortunately, formal learning theory does not lend itself easily to off-the-shelf application. It is difficult to bridge the gap between the laboratory and the classroom. The experimental learning-researcher uses his rats or nonsense syllables or conditioned responses in a highly reductionistic analysis of behavior change; he sacrifices complexity for rigor. The process of molecular analysis is the reverse of the synthesizing efforts of the college student.

The acquisition of knowledge—factual, theoretical, or procedural —by a bright young adult and his changing attitudes and values involve an intricate hierarchy of motives, interacting patterns of specific and general cognitive abilities, the effects of the immediate classroom environment, the intellectual atmosphere of the institution as a whole, and the demands from the community and the social world with which the student identifies himself. The white rat presses the bar in a Skinner box and earns a pellet as a reward, but this tightly controlled event has very few counterparts at the college level. The long-range question for the educational researcher is the immediate task for the teacher: how does one best use the principles of learning and of motivation and personal development for the maximum educational benefits to students?

Learning theory deals with principles of learning in general. It seeks to define the parameters of smooth-function learning curves as the expression of the researcher's nomothetic, abstract interest in a series of otherwise specific events. In contrast, the teacher is concerned with the here-and-now zigzag curve of student learning. In his tutorial relation with students, the instructor is immediately involved with the idiographic pattern of motivation and learning by the individual student as a unique, idiosyncratic, and autonomous person. In this sense the teacher is the mediator between the general principles of learning and their application in a highly specific, if not a unique, learning setting.

The rest of this section is essentially a guide to help the teacher make this transition, that is, to understand those conditions that will, in fact, improve the quantity and the quality of knowledge the student acquires by himself, in the company of his peers, and under the tutelage of his instructor.

Influence of variables. A basic concept in research on learning is the relatively uncomplicated equation *Learning = f (variables)*. However, the universe of variables that can influence the rate and level and direction of learning is almost infinite. It is therefore necessary to seek some degree of systematic ordering by using different subcategories such as environmental variables (class size, teaching style, media), task variables (learning facts, concepts, or attitudes), and individual-difference variables. This third subset comprises those factors provided by the student himself: his motivation, his intelligence, his specific and general aptitudes, his past experiences as a student and as a member of a community. The research literature consistently reports these student-centered factors to be the most important ones determining how rapidly and how well the student will learn and remember.

It is toward these individual-difference variables that the teacher should direct his greater energy in setting the conditions of learning for the individual student. Conventional research on teaching can often be faulted for its excessive involvement with variables having secondary importance for learning. This is why most studies comparing one teaching procedure with a control end up with the usual finding of "no significant differences," for example, between television instruction and live instruction, between large-class lecturing and small-class lecturing, between textbook reading and programmed instruction. A more powerful educational impact can be expected when the teacher is able to release and give greater freedom to those factors that the student himself brings into the classroom.

The change-over from the traditional teaching model to the learning model means, in effect, moving the spotlight from the teacher, and his classic position in center stage, to the student. The teacher stands in the wings where he functions as director, as stage manager, prop man, prompter, and also as a key person viewing and evaluating the student's performance. Since teachers find it difficult to move out of the lectern spotlight, one can expect this form of "teaching" to long endure, logic and data notwithstanding.

Teacher–student–subject-matter interaction. Concern with individual-difference variables is a step forward, but it is not enough; a still finer distinction must be drawn, since students (or teachers or subject-matter areas) refuse to be lumped together and to give uniform responses to a particular change in method of instruction. Some students, for example, prefer strong leadership and dominance by the teacher, while others prefer the permissive environment generated by a warm and friendly teacher. By the same token, some members of the faculty would only embarrass and confuse their students by attempting either the authoritarian or the permissive role. Furthermore, certain curricular offerings almost demand a discussion group (e.g., freshman seminars), while for a different kind of subject matter a large lecture may be adequate.

Added together these variations between students, teachers, and content areas are called *interaction effects.* They are usually subtle and difficult to demonstrate and to quantify in research, but are familiar to the experienced teacher. The transition from an immobile mass-communication system of education to a truly individualized process requires that teachers exercise and utilize these interaction effects. Ideally, instructional arrangements should be sufficiently flexible to meet the nature of individuality and the cognitive style of students who aspire to utilize what they learn for diverse purposes.

Original learning, retention, and transfer. In learning-theory language, the basic model for conducting the educational process is the transfer of learning paradigm:

Group 1 learns A......................transfers to B
Group 2 ....learns only B

In essence, this paradigm states that students who participate in original learning *A* (group 1) will retain this information and use it to their advantage in task *B*, which may occur later in time and in a quite different situation. Control group 2 enters task B without the advantage of prior training in A. Situation A can be almost anything—a specific training program, a particular course of instruction, or the total experience of going to college.

Teachers and students understandably direct their energies toward the acquisition of knowledge (i.e., original learning) during the formal period of the college course and measure this achievement against performance on the final examination. It is then hoped or assumed that the student will carry over appropriate positive (in contrast to negative) transfer effects to his other studies and to his work following graduation. As a subject-matter specialist, a faculty member is primarily interested in organizing and presenting a particular body of knowledge, but as a teacher he must also recognize his responsibilities for planning instruction for the transfer of learning benefits for students. How might this be accomplished?

Historically, the most widely held theory of transfer by college teachers has been the doctrine of formal discipline. It is assumed that the *mental effort* required by the study of certain subjects, for example the classical languages and mathematics, would exercise the student's mental faculties and thereby improve his performance in such other subjects as history, English, and logic.

Transfer of learning has been a topic of experimental investigation and theoretical debate for more than seventy-five years. Differences in teachers, students, and subject matter preclude the specification of an instructional procedure that will be equally applicable to all departments. Furthermore, the mechanics of teaching for transfer are probably less important than the decisions the teacher makes about the objectives and the content of the course, its organization, and the methods used to evaluate student achievement. The classroom is where the learning starts that should later be transferred to other courses and to settings and problems beyond the campus. It is to this kind of learning that the teacher must direct his major attention. When he is satisfied, for example, that the objectives in his course have high and enduring relevance, he has taken the first prerequisite step toward making possible positive transfer benefits by his students. The teacher should feel confident that the material he asks his students to learn is in a form that permits generalization and utilization beyond the classroom.

The student carries the transfer effects in his own head, but he mediates the transfer, not as a side effect of memorizing, drill, and other variations of tedious mental effort, but rather as the result of the *content* he learns and the implications and extensions he can make for utilizing this information. Of particular importance for transfer purposes is that students acquire facility in problem-solving procedures and the use of methodology and knowledge of how to learn. In effect, this means that transfer is brought about through language and the connotations and denotations carried by the symbols, the vocabulary, and the universe of discourse of a particular discipline.

INSTRUCTIONAL OBJECTIVES

To change one's teaching habits and to redefine one's instructional objectives in keeping with the growth of new knowledge is, perhaps, the most significant professional task of the university teacher. The obsolescence of information is a pressing issue for the college teacher, and the setting forth of valid instructional objectives demands the very best talent, if not the prophetic power, of the faculty. It is far more difficult to state instructional objectives in terms of the actual performance of a student after he leaves a course than it is to define *good teaching* in the narrow, information-giving meaning of that term. In comparison with the former, the latter is almost trivial, since telling things to students is hardly more than the first step in the application of learning theory to classroom teaching.

In essence, the matter of course objectives resolves itself into two basic questions: (1) At what time in the future will the relevance of a given fact, procedure, concept, or attitude have passed its inflection point (i.e., half-life) and be starting down the hill toward obsolescence? (2) How can content material be set forth so that the student can tell whether or not he is moving toward the established goals? The ideal instructional objective refers to the changes that are desired in the kinds of questions the student can answer, problems he can solve, procedures he can execute, attitudes he expresses in behavior, and values to which he will aspire.

Clear-cut behavioral objectives are difficult to define for most college-level courses. How, for example, can the instruction *and evaluation* be adjusted to encompass the subtle objectives of motivation to learn, critical thinking, value judgment, favorable attitudes toward the discipline, ability to organize relevant information and to utilize concepts, ability to define and to solve problems, and so forth? Surely these are some of the more pressing and complex educational issues that the subject-matter teacher must meet.

Higher education has never been without its objectives, but the big push to define these in terms of student performance came with the technology of programmed learning developed by B. F. Skinner and his followers.[12] Puristic programmed instruction has been criticized and is indeed vulnerable to the same reservation given to objective tests—the curricular material that lends itself to programming

12. B. F. Skinner, "The Science of Learning and the Art of Teaching."

(or objective testing) too often falls below the fundamental level of understanding and integration that has long stood as the essential goal of teaching. Programmed instruction, in its broader meaning of logical organization, sequencing, and feedback information, probably represents the best single approach toward upgrading the means by which the teacher can help students achieve an explicit educational purpose.

A good mathematics teacher must have been the original instructional programmer. In a not atypical case the professor starts the class hour at the upper left-hand corner of the blackboard, and when the bell rings he has derived or balanced the equation in the lower right-hand corner. The student is expected to learn and to understand the logical sequence from the first term through the successive derivations to the final point. It would seem irrelevant to ask this teacher the terminal behavior expected of his students other than that they be able to "understand and to reproduce and to handle the extensions of this sample of mathematical logic."

A similar argument could be used for most college courses—namely, that sequential ordering of information is itself an instructional objective—and it would seem picayune, if not redundant and belabored, to restate this objective in behavioral terms and in reference to various external performance situations. Bright students who have been acquiring facts and procedural information and understanding concepts from poorly written textbooks for a long time have been able to retrieve and utilize this information when necessary after the course is over. There is no question that the instructional process can be improved by applying the programmed-learning model, but the solution does not rest in adapting all printed instructional material to the programmed-learning format or some close variation of it.

As one step toward achieving greater specificity of course objectives, it may be helpful for the teacher to inventory the substance of his course in a few familiar categories. The teaching and evaluation procedures for each of these categories call for a distinctive approach.

Accumulation of factual information. The ability to retrieve an impressive array of facts is not necessarily the measure of an educated man, although students do tend to give higher ratings to teachers who stress the learning of specific factual information. This attitude is to be expected since, for the most part, education has been dominated by pressures to learn new facts as a means of answering rather specific questions. One of the main troubles with a "fact" is the disconcerting way it becomes a nonfact in a short period of time. Nevertheless, since facts are prerequisite to understanding concepts, principles, and generalizations, each student must necessarily start to construct his hierarchy of knowledge in a given field on a factual foundation.

Meaningfulness is the key variable in learning facts, since only rote-learned items that become meaningful remain in memory and carry a utility function over time and through variations as the student moves from place to place and from problem to problem. In order to achieve meaningfulness, which is personal and subjective, the student must actively participate in the process of learning what the facts mean. Writing a term paper, conducting a special project, or discussing an idea in a group contributes to this purpose.

Acquisition of skills. Skill-learning is a commonplace process, which demonstrates the basic conditions for learning and retention. However, displaying finger dexterity or acquiring complicated perceptual-motor skills is less important in the liberal arts undergraduate curriculum than in several areas of vocational training. For the most part, the extensions of research and theory on verbal learning in the classroom have greater relevance to college teaching than do the findings from studies on motor skills. Nevertheless, it should be noted, for instance, that the conditions which cause a student to retain a skill over time—active participation, feedback, and the like—are also the conditions that make it difficult to change it.

Understanding concepts and generalizations. It is usually more difficult to teach the meaning of abstract ideas than to lecture about specific factual information. Considerably more is known about the teaching of substantive material, whether it be facts or taxonomic concepts, than about the teaching of problem-solving procedures and research methods. Here, indeed, is the nub of the task. It is easier for the chemistry professor, for example, to teach laboratory technics and the facts of chemistry than to teach theory and the complex methods of research. Despite this difficulty, formal education in the future will necessarily place greater emphasis on methodology, concepts, generalizations, principles, and their utilization than on the teaching of informational specifics.

The two fundamental pedagogical problems involved in teaching concepts are (1) how to teach abstract concepts without divorcing the student from the logic, the objective data, and the concrete real-world references that support these ideas and (2) how to teach for the future utilization of conceptual knowledge in a problem-solving or decision-making setting outside the classroom.

The concepts that a student learns are not packaged units of information to be acquired and stored in memory like books in a library. He should be able to draw on his understanding of concepts for general use from one class to another and in the natural setting away from school. The teacher contributes to the student's understanding of concepts in many ways, but at least three guidelines can be mentioned as appropriate for the kind of learning that usually occurs in a college course.

1. The material the student reads, studies, and hears must be organized by the teacher into a logical hierarchy. The teacher must establish the basic organizational sequence and structure that will enable the student to acquire the kind of knowledge that carries some degree of generality beyond the classroom. This is programming in its generic sense.

2. "Students learn only what they do" is one of the tried and true clichés in learning theory. It is oversimplified, of course, but it does highlight the importance of active participation by the learner in generating specific examples and instances that either confirm or deny the meaning of an abstract concept. With each of these examples the student is testing his understanding of the concept and its boundaries, and the teacher, of course, is usually the one to judge how adequate is the meaning the student has acquired.

3. Knowledge of results, feedback, or reinforcement is viewed by many learning theorists as a prerequisite for learning. When a student makes a response, reaches a conclusion, or makes a decision, he needs to know the rightness or wrongness of what he has done. The college student is an intelligent person who can bridge time and can also respond to subtle cues; thus he does not require the flash of a green light or a piece of candy or a nickel as an immediate reward for his own response. He can be rewarded by the confidence that comes with knowing he understands what he is reading. It would, however, be rather difficult for reinforcement to occur as the student proceeds through his assignment if he did not know what he was supposed to learn or could not see that he was moving in the right direction. This means that prior to the effective use of reinforcement, the teacher must identify and state the instructional objectives in a language and form that are clear to the student.[13]

Changing attitudes and values. As mentioned earlier, most academic departments accept attitude change, value formation, and the acquisition of new and stronger educational motives, ambitions, and aspirations as appropriate and legitimate instructional objectives. The affective domain is difficult to define and cannot be taught in the usual direct, preceptive way. Students are probably influenced more by the example the instructor sets than by his platform sermons.

The extensive research of social scientists on the analysis of attitudes and values can provide the teacher with valuable background information. *The American College* is a classic example of a growing

13. Stanford C. Ericksen, "Education for Transfer of Learning in a Changing Environment."

body of knowledge about the personal and social development of the college student and about the influences on what and how he learns.[14]

In puristic, objective terms, an attitude requires some form of behavioral expression as evidence that a change has occurred. Paper-and-pencil or verbal assent may not reveal the degree to which a new attitude will actually take form as a change in behavior. The most convincing evidence will very likely be given outside the classroom, probably at a later date. The teacher is, therefore, usually limited to working with attitudes at the verbal level, talking and writing about attitudes and values that are intrinsically related to the course objectives.

TRANSMITTING INFORMATION

Since a college teacher must write his own how-to-do-it specifics on transmitting information, this section simply will point out the chief uses and the pitfalls and regressions that characterize the several modes of instruction.

The lecture. To McKeachie "the lecture is the newspaper or journal of teaching; it, more than any other teaching, must be up-to-date." [15] Mass-printing techniques have placed the book within reach of almost every student, and yet teachers have successfully resisted the suggestion that the fact-filled lecture might now be obsolete. And they have been encouraged in their tenacity by cost-conscious administrators whose major interest is the logistical "efficiency" of the large lecture. The lecture, despite its instructional vulnerability, has become for many professors a security blanket without which they would neither feel like teachers nor be so recognized by their students. Such is the power of tradition.

A good lecture offers special educational advantages. In addition to updating texts, the lecturer can reemphasize those points which he feels are most pertinent to the course objectives. He can synthesize different topics and new material that threaten to overwhelm his students; he can provide the structure within which students can organize what they learn.

Students are naturally curious; they enjoy learning new things and find rewards in mastering new concepts or developing new skills. Studies on college learning indicate, for instance, that when lectures are arranged around questions which pique students' interest, rather than around mere recitations of fact, not only is learning improved but interest in further learning about a topic is increased.[16] In particu-

14. Nevitt Sanford, *The American College.*
15. Wilbert J. McKeachie, "New Developments in Teaching."
16. D. E. Berlyne, *Conflict, Arousal, and Curiosity.*

lar, questions which arouse students' curiosity about novel aspects of things already familiar to them may have significant influence on the development of curiosity.

Perhaps the most crucial element in the good lecture is the personality and the attitude of the instructor himself. A lecturer with style and flair—or an honest enthusiasm for his subject—may well be able to inspire his students to further work in his field. He may be able to turn some students on—and others off. The public image of the master teacher has to a large extent been based on teachers with this motivational or inspirational quality. Student popularity-polls of good teaching are heavily weighted toward the teacher who has the ability to maintain interest, to excite and challenge, and to arouse students through the substance of the discipline or its social relevance. This ability to stir up students may indeed be the central value of a good lecture, but it must go beyond mere showmanship and crass entertainment, for most students will see through and reject a contrived attempt at happiness-through-learning.[17]

The seminar and the discussion group. Small classes can satisfy many of the requirements for student motivation, learning, and thinking; and their long-term future in higher education seems assured. A seminar course is quite likely to involve students more deeply in the subject matter than does the conventional discussion group, but both are misused by the instructor who chooses the small forum as a stage for his lecture.

McKeachie has summarized the particular advantages of the discussion class:

1. to give students opportunities to formulate principles in their own words and to suggest applications of these principles;
2. to help students become aware of and to define problems based on information derived from readings or lectures;
3. to gain acceptance for information or theories counter to folklore or previous beliefs of students;
4. to get feedback on how well his instructional objectives are being attained.[18]

It is difficult for a teacher to lead a successful discussion group because he must recognize and manage the contrasting motives, interests, and concerns of the individual students while maintaining progress toward his content objectives and avoiding the tendency to drift into an unproductive bull session. As educational technology grows, inde-

17. Stanford C. Ericksen, "The Lecture."
18. Wilbert J. McKeachie, "The Discussion Group."

pendent study and self-instructional facilities will become more generally used, and the discussion group will form the essential supporting base for such arrangements.

Small classes are expensive to operate, and other than the use of teaching assistants or student-led groups, no obvious means of reducing costs seems to exist.[19] The skills of the effective discussion-leader differ somewhat from those of the large-class lecturer. High-level competence in subject matter may not always be required, especially if discussion is tied in with a large class or if, by some other means, it follows the curricular organization established by an experienced teacher.

The laboratory. Laboratory instruction is also expensive, yet most science teachers favor early and continued student exposure to the laboratory. The instructor must be particularly careful to define the educational objectives of *laboratory* instruction, which is essentially a form of independent study with readily available tutorial help.

Laboratory teachers should be alert to the drift toward factual learning and procedural mechanics that is being made at the sacrifice of the analytical and conceptual aspects of instruction and the freedom for individual inquiry. The audiotutorial laboratory course developed by Professor Postlethwait and his associates at Purdue University is an impressive combination of educational technology and careful instructional planning, designed to achieve some measure of individualization in an otherwise large lecture-laboratory course.[20] However, its value would lessen if students were locked into a predetermined track of factual learning or had minimal options for independent study of particular phenomena that challenge their interests and abilities. The undergraduate laboratory, automated or not, should include the possibility of open-ended inquiry by each student, permitting him to branch off from the main line at several points throughout the term.

The field trip. The large universities may have populated themselves out of the field trip as a routine instructional arrangement. It requires altogether too much money and logistical effort to manage a group of 200 to 800 students on a controlled off-campus visit. Two developments may have further outmoded the field trip for college students. (1) Technology makes it possible to send a camera crew into the field to bring back into the large class carefully selected and edited samples of concrete issues, problems, and procedures, which are directly relevant to a course. (2) Simulations and games, now being developed for instructional use, hold high promise for helping students

19. C. Leuba, "Using Groups in Independent Study."
20. S. N. Postlethwait, Harvey D. Telinde, and David Husband, *Introduction to Plant Science.*

identify, interact with, and manage various aspects of a complex event or relationship.

The interchange between academia and the community is today so important that the printed case-study or the once-in-a-while field trip can hardly be an adequate contribution to the new educational goals. Mental health, poverty, environmental decay, traffic, urban problems, and so forth are altogether too important to be looked at by the student in simple spectator fashion. Systematic and intensive field experience is becoming a more common aspect of otherwise traditional liberal arts courses in the social sciences.[21]

Interdisciplinary and independent study. Interdisciplinary efforts characteristically face the problem of central instructional responsibility. If it is difficult to define instructional objectives for one's own course, it becomes doubly so for curricular offerings conceived by a committee. The educational benefits to the student must be more explicit than "offers an enriching learning experience." Interdisciplinary programs and independent study should give students considerable freedom for decision making and self-defined educational objectives.

In its least acceptable form, independent study turns students free for a period of time prior to giving them a required comprehensive examination. This practice amounts to ruthless exploitation of the student's extrinsic motivation to succeed or to conform by studying only what the faculty requires that he study. The essential value of independent study is the motivational freedom allowed the student to select a topic of personal interest and to pursue it at the rate and in the manner compatible with his personal methods of study and his abilities. Between these two extremes many variations of independent study and self-instructional arrangements are possible, as instructors seek to cope with the many constraints on their freedom to work with students as individuals.

Remedial instruction. Teaching the bottom half of the class is a revealing measurement of one's competence as an instructor. The slow student—whether he is so for reasons of motivation, ability, or personal, educational, or social background—should have direct access to the educational resources of an institution and should receive at least as much attention from the faculty as the superior student in the privileged honors program. Since the latter is well equipped to follow an independent-study course, perhaps the time, money, and talent now set aside for honors programs should be redirected toward remedial instruction for the bottom 25 percent of the student body.

Unfortunately, remedial instruction is not attractive to most college teachers and is offered only when a student is visibly in trouble.

21. Richard Mann, "Field Study in the Inner City" and "Project OUTREACH."

Many of the students who are now confused would have been better served had an early diagnostic evaluation been made of their strong and weak points. Instructors should know more about each student's position at the start of the rat-race-for-grades so that they might apply the proper handicaps.

A systematic program of remedial instruction calls for (1) diagnostic assessment when students start a new course of study, (2) easy access to remedial help from instructors or from special study materials, (3) motivational support through counseling or small group discussions, with particular emphasis on recognition and reward for progress.

TECHNOLOGICAL TEACHING AIDS

The term *educational technology* usually refers to such mechanical and electronic devices as slides, motion pictures, television, audio tape-recorders, 8mm single-concept films, and, more recently, the computer. The computer is the only teaching machine with a future, and like these other technological aids it will be successful only insofar as instructional content is carefully defined and organized (programmed) by teaching specialists in subject-matter fields. The conventional audiovisual aids are used primarily to manipulate the stimulus with little concern for the student's own mediating processes and his response. In closed-circuit television, for example, the image of the instructor making a classroom presentation is magnified manyfold and distributed to as many outlets as can be tied into the system. The student's source of the stimulus material has simply been transferred from the professor himself to the television monitor.

The presentation of curricular material by technological devices does not relieve the instructor from his overall responsibility for integrating instructional objectives, teaching procedures, and methods for evaluating student progress. Other than its novelty effect, the "innovative" use of media may contribute little to the quality of instruction unless the media are selected by the teacher because of their special potential for helping students make the finer discriminations related to a particular aspect of the subject matter and its meaning.

Because of high capital costs and technical servicing requirements, most of the electronic instructional aids are centrally controlled in audiovisual, television, and computing centers and in libraries. Their optimal educational use, however, calls for decentralized adaptation by the individual teacher and, to a certain extent, by the students. The interdependence of objectives, teaching (and media used in teaching), and evaluation is shown in the following summary of the more familiar forms of educational technology.

The *book* is probably the most powerful and widely used technological aid, but judging from student complaints that, in effect, a textbook makes formal classroom lectures redundant if not obsolete, it is still frequently underused. Updated printed instructional materials are now becoming available in less expensive forms such as paperbacks and locally reproduced copy.

The *blackboard* has strong survival value. Its widespread use over so many years is evidence that visual images of words and diagrams are important components of teaching. This test of time suggests that high fidelity in the visual image is not always a particularly significant specification for good instruction. Line drawings and schematics often contribute just as much to the learning process as detailed reproductions on film or slides.

The magic lantern gradually gave way to *slides,* to the *filmstrip, overhead projections,* and *motion pictures.* Instructors today seem to prefer the moving image (film or video tape)—probably because a moving picture seems to have a certain amount of attention-holding power—even where motion is not particularly relevant or essential to the substantive content. *Video tape,* now cheaper than 16mm film, permits the instructor to experiment with various forms of visual presentation. The television medium is thus becoming decentralized—as all media should be.

The *audio tape-recorder* is essentially a form of decentralized educational radio. Dial-access systems have been introduced at a number of colleges and universities, and for such subjects as music, speech, language, and literature, a library listening room is a valuable instructional resource. Frequently, however, these innovations serve logistical, rather than specific, instructional purposes. This often happens when an instructional system is introduced by the administration, by media men, or systems engineers with inadequate faculty consultation over the specific functions required by the course objectives, the methods for evaluating student achievement, and the tie-in with the several nonsystem teaching procedures.

Once the problem of compatibility between machines and formats has been solved, the *8mm single-concept, closed-loop film* will be widely used. In the meantime, the number and the educational value of available films remain limited for particular content areas .In principle the cartridged film is relatively foolproof. A student can now study filmed material in the library or in his private study-space with the same flexibility he might exercise in reading a library book. He is in control of a learning situation and can adapt his rate of progress, his review, and his self-testing procedures to his personal habits of learning and to his own peculiar strengths and weaknesses.

The college student of the future will have access to the computer-controlled, independent-study carrel, where, literally speaking, a world of knowledge will be at his fingertips. What knowledge is worth knowing? will no longer be a rhetorical question but a central issue in the seminars and discussion groups that must be closely associated with these self-instructional arrangements.

Computer-assisted instruction (CAI) is still in the drawing-board stage. Software development—meaning, in this instance, the curricular content and its use by students—lags behind hardware development, and estimates differ widely on when the computer-mediated teaching machine will be operational at the college level. The full educational value of this expensive but powerful technology will depend on whether the subject-matter teacher is willing to devote his time and interest to putting something worthwhile into the machine in a form that can be used effectively by his students.

Simulation is a form of educational technology, which may or may not involve special devices and equipment. The instructor seeks to duplicate (i.e., simulate) certain features of a physical, social, or conceptual environment in a manner that will give the student direct exposure to these preselected features under controlled circumstances. Thus the teacher's first step in planning a simulation project is to identify the particular real-world feature that he wishes to highlight for his students. Second, he must be sure that each student exercises some degree of control over the sequence of events; the student must be an active participant rather than a passive observer. A third critical element in simulation generally follows almost automatically from steps one and two, namely, the return of information to the student regarding the consequences of his action, decision, or inaction.[22]

The instructional pros and cons of educational technology—its procedures (e.g., programmed learning, simulation) and devices (video tapes, computers, etc.)—could go on at length. The literature is heavy with oversells and cautions, with theories and experiments, with exhortations and cynicisms. But when all is said and done, the classroom teacher remains the central decision-maker regarding those conditions that support the acquisition of knowledge and attitude change by his particular students.

Equally important, however, is the teacher's responsibility and his authority for evaluating student achievement and, where necessary, assigning grades. To many teachers this final step is nearly always a petty, contrived, and onerous task, but one that nevertheless cannot be farmed out to others. Like it or not, teachers must concern themselves with the matter of testing and grading.

22. Stanford C. Ericksen, "Simulation."

EVALUATION

Evaluation is a sensitive and delicate topic, and teachers know that error is partner to passing judgment on the quality of student performance. It is difficult to make objective evaluative decisions within the complexities of the classroom, the teaching laboratory, the field setting, or the independent-study program. Generally, students do not object so much to hard work as they do to unfair treatment, and it is in matters of evaluation that this question of educational justice is most clearly posed.

The demands involved in systematic evaluation of student performance often tempt teachers to resort to ready-made, commercially available measuring devices. It is, of course, perfectly legitimate to use a technically sound external evaluating instrument in lieu of a teacher-made test, provided that the teacher *neither compromises nor modifies his instructional objectives to fit the requirements of the available test.* In most instances, however, the extra effort required of the teacher to develop a set of evaluation procedures for his own course will most likely yield a valid instrument which measures student progress toward his short- and long-term instructional objectives.

EVALUATION OF INSTRUCTION

Student evaluations can be a valuable resource for the teacher critically assessing his own effectiveness and the educational goals he sets for his students. Research shows that student evaluations provide useful information on at least three aspects of a course: (1) the personal effectiveness of the instructor, (2) the rapport between instructor and student, (3) the organization and management of a particular class. Some studies suggest that teacher characteristics associated in the minds of students with effective instruction remain stable over time—a professor judged favorably a few years ago will likely receive about the same rating today. However, stereotypes about "good teaching" are undoubtedly changing. Findings indicate that students are able to make clear discriminations: they upgrade ratings of younger teachers who publish research articles, give better ratings to small than large classes, and prefer classes involving considerable group participation and a high degree of student-teacher contact. On the other hand, neither difficulty of the course as perceived by the student nor the grade he receives seems to be related to the way he evaluates the teacher himself in contrast to the objectives and the substance of a particular course.

The instructor must be careful to adjust the interpretation he gives to the student ratings in the light of at least three frequent sources of distortion: (1) the wording of the questionnaire, (2) the halo effect—the student's tendency to be uncritically generous in his evaluation, (3) a biased sample caused by failure of some students to return the questionnaire.

Apart from systematic and formal ratings from students, the teacher might on occasion stand back and take a self-critical view of his teaching methods, his course objectives, and the extent to which students have realized them. Carefully made examinations given during the course will indicate how thoroughly students are grasping the subgoals of the course as well as what alterations in method and content need to be made. When the teacher is trying to judge himself, diagnostic information inferred or given directly by the spontaneous behavior of individual students is probably more significant than some sort of Nielsen rating of the teacher as a mass communicator.

GRADING SYSTEMS

Controversies about college grading systems develop when grades are interpreted as universal indices of academic proficiency. In fact, they are never much more than simplistic expressions of the extremely complicated interaction of teacher, student, and a body of knowledge. Their interpretation requires external references, for example, the teacher's judgment of student achievement or the level of student performance in competition with others. Whether or not the assignment of grades on a unidimensional scale is worth the trouble and conflict is a question which is now being asked more and more often by teachers, students, and administrators. Whatever the decisions, they should not be lightly made since criterion measures in education inevitably influence the curriculum and instructional program of an institution.

Conventional grading. The administrative and social aspects of grading are matters of far-reaching concern. Grade records are reviewed and compared by prospective employers or admissions committees and are used as a basis for special awards, eligibility, and the like. These administrative uses of the conventional grading system stand at least one step outside the classroom and are too easily subject to misuse and exploitation. For example, teachers should strongly object to the use of the grading system as a device for controlling nonacademic behavior, such as tardiness or absenteeism or disruption. If the system is used for this purpose, teachers should disclaim the meaning of the grade as a measure of academic achievement.

Most important for consideration here is the place of grading in the instructional process: How do grades help students learn? Grading procedures, whatever they may be, should first be judged in terms of their educational influence on the student. Some critics, looking at the effect of the present grading system on the student-teacher relationship, hold that the student's work is neither willing nor independent when it is done under the threat of testing by the same person who sets the learning task. Other critics charge professors with using grades to promote conformity among students.[23]

Challenges are also being made to the opinion that grades motivate students to learn. If grades in college are analogous to salaries in jobs, if good grades are the only satisfaction students receive, if students have no feeling of accomplishment or sense of capability, education is in a sorry fix indeed.

> Creativity in learning is best facilitated when self-criticism and self-evaluation are basic, and evaluation by others is of secondary importance. . . . The best research organizations, in industry as well as in the academic world, have learned that external evaluation is largely fruitless if the goal is creative work. The individual must be permitted to make his own efforts.[24]

Coupled with the notion that the motivation to earn a grade produces weak educational results is the charge that the type of learning it encourages is not particularly relevant today. Traditionally education has stressed the assimilation of an established body of information and students were graded accordingly. But, it is argued, "factual" information is now rapidly outdated; the more important instructional objective is helping students learn how to learn, a goal which is difficult to measure with objective tests and conventional grades.

Pass-fail grading. Critics of established grading procedures have advanced a number of alternatives; pass-fail (or better, pass-incomplete) is the "in" system today. Essentially, pass-fail reduces the options available to the teacher for scoring student achievement from infinite (the 0–100 numerical system) or the standard five (A, B, C, D, E) to only two. Such a minimal system of evaluation, supported by descriptive statements by instructors, might reduce the current emphasis on grade-grubbing, which alienates student from teacher and promotes learning, not to satisfy individual needs, capacities, and curiosity, but rather to meet the instructor's expectations. Pass-fail, its proponents claim, will supplant motivation to earn grades with motivation to seek knowledge and understanding for their own sake.

Pass-fail presents a major administrative problem in the evaluation of student academic performance for graduate school admission, transfer, honors, and so forth. However, in 1967 more than seventy colleges and universities throughout the country were using the pass-

---

23. Stuart Miller, *Measure, Number, and Weight.*
24. Carl Rogers, "The Facilitation of Significant Learning," p. 12.

fail system in one form or another, and the number of schools is increasing each year.

Little hard data to support either the claims of its adherents or the disavowals of its detractors are yet available from these trials. It appears from preliminary reports, however, that the transition from conventional grading systems to pass-fail is accompanied by a period of adjustment during which students may retain their grade-oriented behavior or attempt to take advantage of the new system by loafing. At the University of Michigan, for example, after a year of allowing juniors and seniors to opt one pass-fail course outside their major or required courses, student performance-levels were closely related to general academic abilities as measured by cumulative grade-point averages. Obviously the A and B students have little experience in studying for C's, even when relieved from the pressure of having to do well.

EXAMINATION PROCEDURES

When the authoritarian college professor of former years made his platform pronouncements, he was speaking absolute truth, and his judgment of a student's achievement was accepted without overt questioning. But today students and faculty alike are asking for more information about the evaluation of academic progress. The criteria for grading and the procedures for testing are seen as matters to be identified and discussed as open and empirical problems. A good case can be made for the argument that there is more room for improvement in our evaluation procedures than in any other single aspect of a teacher's task.

Grading criteria. Teachers are faced with two general bases for grading, absolute standards and relative standards. The use of the absolute standard requires, in its ideal form, that a teacher formulate his major and minor objectives and then devise some means of telling when a student has achieved them. Normally, he simply compares the student's response with his own judgment about what the student should have said or written and grades accordingly.

Resistance to grading on the basis of absolute standards, which are often unreasonable and idiosyncratic, has led to the widespread practice of using relative standards in which a student's standing with respect to other members of his class determines his grade. The system of grading on the curve presumes that usually a class will contain a representative sample of students and that the performance of the middle range can serve to define the C, or average, grade. A teacher who assigns grades in this way must have in mind some ideal grade distribution, and schemes of various kinds—some rather elaborate—

are worked out to fit students' performance measurements to whatever distribution is sought.

No fully satisfactory method of grading has yet been found; the best policy is probably a compromise between relative and absolute methods. Setting up clear standards of proficiency, with latitude for modification as indicated by general aptitude tests or other criteria, is likely to prove most acceptable to all concerned. In large courses made up of representative groups of students, it is probably best to have an approximate grade-distribution as a controlling standard.[25]

The objective examination. Glaciers melt, but the slow momentum of academic change means that new instructors should be prepared to spend many hours putting together objective examinations or grading essay tests.

The construction of objective tests and their evaluation as measuring instruments have become a technical specialty, and these pages can in no way be considered a test maker's manual. The present summary simply highlights again the necessary involvement of the teacher in establishing the internal consistency among instructional objectives, teaching procedures, and methods of evaluation. Vague statements of good instructional intentions cannot be tested unambiguously. In order to evaluate students during a course, the instructor must set forth his immediate objective, that is, a statement of what the student should be able to do as a consequence of his learning. "Although most tests only sample the present competence of a student, good test items provide some prediction of how well the student might perform at a later date or in a different situation. . . . Immediate objectives should be chosen to approximate as nearly as possible the long-term goals of the course."[26]

Several types of objective tests are available to the teacher. The best known, the multiple-choice test, has been criticized for measuring only the recognition of factual material, but it is possible to write multiple-choice test items and other types which provide reliable measures of a student's ability to understand concepts and apply principles. Testing specialists frequently proclaim that objective items can be constructed to measure most of the course goals normally assessed by the essay examination. The ingenuity of skilled test makers in support of this claim is fair evidence that the evaluation potential of the objective examination is rarely achieved.

Some of the less widely known forms of test questions retain the scoring objectivity of the multiple-choice format while allowing some of the creative or individualistic response usually associated with the

25. John Milholland, "The Assignment of Grades."
26. Karl L. Zinn, "Testing Academic Achievement."

essay type. Computer-controlled testing will extend and improve this capability by evaluating the student's ability to ask appropriate questions in problem situations. For example, medical students are given a description of a patient's symptoms and are required to indicate what questions they would ask in making a diagnosis. After being given answers to their questions, the students proceed toward a final diagnosis.

The essay examination. The evaluation of thinking, creativity, and understanding is usually made with the essay examination, a test in which the student is graded on how well he can organize information and express opinions as measured against the considered judgments of his teacher. Long-standing evidence from several sources suggests that the prospect of an essay test leads the student to a pattern of study activity that emphasizes the organization and the interrelationships of facts and principles, whereas the prospect of an objective test leads to memorization of details. These expectations do not, however, reflect an intrinsic difference between the two modes of testing.

The essay examination can range from a series of short, fill-in-the-blanks to a two-hour or longer writing assignment on a single topic. The weakness in this method of testing is not in the form of the questions or their purpose but, rather, in the low reliability of the scoring. Many potential troubles are minimized if tests are planned carefully. The teacher should frame questions at a level consistent with that of most students in the class, state the questions with sufficient clarity and detail to insure that each student will work the same problem, specify any restrictions on scope and length of answers, and select questions to provide an adequate sample of the instructional objectives.

Most of the criticism of essay testing concerns the lack of consistency in grading, not only by different readers but also by a single examiner. A few general guidelines about the mechanics of reading bluebooks can help to reduce the discrepancy in scoring. Teachers who use essay examinations should, for instance, (1) insure that new readers receive supervised practice in scoring tests, (2) score each paper without knowing who wrote it, (3) grade all answers to one question at one sitting, and (4) read the bluebooks in random sequence.

A common practice among experienced teachers is to judge each essay question analytically by assigning points to various sections. These subscores or marginal comments by the reader can be helpful to the student but may not be necessary steps in reaching the total score. A few studies indicate, however, that teachers generally rely more on "cold-turkey" recognition of quality than on attempts to be analytically systematic.

It is not necessary to draw rigid boundaries between essay and objective examinations. The teacher's problem is to develop whatever methods of testing will sample a student's achievement of complex educational objectives rather than his competence as a memorizer of facts and details. Undue emphasis on a particular technique of testing (or teaching) is a pitfall into which all teachers may slip occasionally.

The oral examination. The ultimate essay examination is the face-to-face interview where an examiner assesses the substance of a student's comments as well as any elements of style and personal characteristics that he may judge to be significant. Oral examinations are often used in honors programs where the student is examined by a group of professors from his own institution or from other schools. The prospect and the experience of an oral encounter frequently produce considerable anxiety in the student and, as a consequence, may result in an inferior display of what he knows and the way he thinks. One of the chronic problems of the oral examination, however, lies with the examiners; this is especially true if their differences of opinion encourage them to role play for one another rather than to focus on the student himself. An oral examination does permit the teacher to pursue in greater depth some aspect of a student's response and to note his personal manner and the various forms of nonverbal communication which may be pertinent to his academic achievement and his prospects for further study.

Where an oral examination is used on a regular basis, members of the examining committee should prepare guidelines, study and discuss them, and agree on those to be used before they confront the student. Following the examination, committee members should make independent ratings but should always be free to modify them in the light of the group discussion reaching, hopefully, a consensus.

Term papers and special projects. For some experienced teachers, the preferred method for formal evaluation of students is the term paper, the essay, or the special project. Here it is important that students have freedom to select a topic for analysis or at least to choose from a list of topics. The advantage of this freedom is motivational—to permit the student to come as close as possible to working on a document that reflects what he wants to do and that, therefore, carries with it the advantages that accrue from a positive, aggressive, and interested attack on the problem. Some teachers, at least for intermediate and advanced courses taken by juniors and seniors, would rather spend the extra time reading and evaluating these reports than devote considerable man-hours to the preparation of a valid objective examination. If a teacher is professionally competent to offer these courses, he is also qualified to evaluate the quality of individual papers on diverse subjects written in various styles.

Diagnostic evaluation. Instructors generally pay much more attention to the level of student achievement at the end of the course than they do to the student's standing at the beginning. The fulfillment of formal prerequisite course-requirements is no guarantee that a student has achieved the level of content proficiency required to enter a course. It generally can be assumed that for a typical class the bottom 25 percent of the students start out handicapped by inadequate information, skill, knowledge, and the like. These students should be identified and, if conditions permit, a remedial or tutorial section or other opportunities should be provided for them. Otherwise many of them will fall farther and farther behind as the course proceeds and in the end will display the familiar signs of frustration: having never been able to keep up with a course, they transfer or fail.

Corrective action by the instructor will probably most help the student when provided at the beginning of a course. It might be quite revealing to a new instructor to give his final examination, on an experimental basis, on the first day of the course. This diagnostic procedure gives the instructor and the students useful information on what topics and areas need special attention.

Proficiency evaluation. Proficiency testing is well established and widely used in such areas as mathematics and modern language. However, the extension of this principle to other disciplines has been rather limited. To section a large class of entering freshmen in the traditional History of Western Civilization on the basis of general scholastic aptitude or high school grades seems a less-valid procedure than to section these students on the basis of their actual knowledge of history. The same argument could apply to other areas in which introductory course-material is given in high school.

The practice of permitting students to progress through selected parts of the curriculum on a proficiency basis will be more frequently used in the years ahead. It marks a significant advance in using the educational resources that lie in the particular backgrounds and the differential abilities and motivations of the students themselves. For his part, the teacher will make the distinctive contribution of a subject-matter specialist by defining the appropriate standards for achieving the educational objectives that make his course worthwhile. In many ways this is the ideal educational arrangement: it plays to the strength of the student and to the disciplinary competence of the teacher, and it places teaching qua teaching in proper perspective as the mediating process between a student and a body of knowledge with its supporting values.

Works Cited

Astin, A. W. *The College Environment*. Washington: American Council on Education, 1968.

———. "Undergraduate Institutions and the Production of Scientists." *Science* 141 (1963): 334-38.

Berlyne, D. E. *Conflict, Arousal, and Curiosity*. New York: McGraw-Hill Book Co., 1960.

Brown, Donald R. "Student Stress and the Institutional Environment." *Journal of Social Issues* 23 (1967): 92-107.

Bruner, Jerome S. *The Process of Education*. Cambridge: Harvard University Press, 1960.

Ericksen, Stanford C. "Education for Transfer of Learning in a Changing Environment." *Journal of Dental Education* 31 (1967): 342-47.

———. "An Experimental Study of Individual Differences in Scholastic Motives." *Journal of Educational Psychology* (1940): 507-16.

———. "The Lecture." Memo to the Faculty, no. 30. Ann Arbor: Center for Research on Learning and Teaching, 1968.

———. "Simulation." Memo to the Faculty, no. 19. Ann Arbor: Center for Research on Learning and Teaching, 1966.

Fader, Daniel N., and Schaevitz, Morton H. *Hooked on Books*. New York: Berkley Publishing Corp., Medallion Books, 1966.

Feldman, Kenneth A., and Newcomb, Theodore M. *The Impacts of College on Students*. San Francisco: Jossey-Bass, 1969.

Holland, J. L. "Determinants of College Choice." *College and University* 34 (1959): 11-28.

Koen, Frank. "The Training of Graduate Student Teaching Assistants." *Educational Record*, winter 1968, pp. 92-102.

Leuba, C. "Using Groups in Independent Study." *Antioch College Reports*, no. 5 (1963).

McKeachie, Wilbert J. "The Discussion Group." Memo to the Faculty, no. 14. Ann Arbor: Center for Research on Learning and Teaching, 1965.

———. "Motivation, Teaching Methods, and College Learning." In *Nebraska Symposium on Motivation, 1961*, edited by M. R. Jones. Lincoln, Neb.: University of Nebraska Press, 1962.

———. "New Developments in Teaching." Report for Higher Education Literature Search Project. Washington: U.S. Office of Education, 1966.

McKee, John M. "The Draper Experiment: A Programmed Learning Project." In *Trends in Programmed Instruction*, edited by Gabriel D. Ofiesh and Wesley C. Meierhenry. Washington: Department of Audiovisual Instruction, National Education Association, 1964.

Mann, Richard. "Field Study in the Inner City." *Development and Experiment in College Teaching* 5 (1969): 26.

———. "Project OUTREACH: An Innovation in Teaching Introductory Psychology." *Development and Experiment in College Teaching* 2 (1966): 14.

Milholland, John. "The Assignment of Grades." Memo to the Faculty, no. 4. Ann Arbor: Center for Research on Learning and Teaching, 1964.

Miller, Stuart. *Measure, Number, and Weight: A Polemical Statement of the College Grading Problem*. Ann Arbor: Center for Research on Learning and Teaching, 1967.

O'Connor, Patricia. "Motivation to Learn." Memo to the Faculty, no. 7. Ann Arbor: Center for Research on Learning and Teaching, 1964.

Postlethwait, S. N.; Telinde, Harvey D.; and Husband, David G. *Introduction to Plant Science*. Minneapolis: Burgess Publishing Co., 1966.

Rogers, Carl. "The Facilitation of Significant Learning." In *Instruction: Some Contemporary Viewpoints*, edited by L. Siegel. San Francisco: Chandler Publishing Co., 1967.

Sanford, Nevitt, ed. *The American College*. New York: John Wiley & Sons, 1962.

——. *Where Colleges Fail*. San Francisco: Jossey-Bass, 1967.

Scully, Malcolm G. "Academic Turmoil Grows over Moves to 'Politicize' Universities, Associations." *Chronicle of Higher Education*, 13 January 1969.

Skinner, B. F. "The Science of Learning and the Art of Teaching." *Harvard Education Review* 24 (1954): 86-97.

——. *The Technology of Teaching*. New York: Appleton-Century-Crofts, 1968.

Thistlethwaite, D. L. "College Press and Changes in Study Plans of Talented Students." *Journal of Educational Psychology* 51 (1960): 222-34.

Wunsch, Ellis. "The Pilot Project: An Attack on Impersonality and Academic Isolation in a Large College." Memo to the Faculty, no. 20. Ann Arbor: Center for Research on Learning and Teaching, 1966.

Zinn, Karl L. "Testing Academic Achievement." Memo to the Faculty, no. 5. Ann Arbor: Center for Research on Learning and Teaching, 1964.

Teaching Styles
in the Humanities

JOSEPH AXELROD

"The social revolution in this country demands new educational procedures and perhaps new educational content," James R. Squire recently told an audience of English professors at a Modern Language Association meeting. Mr. Squire believes the discipline-centered approach in the field of English has now run its course and "some new educational crusade is about to replace it." [1]

The new educational crusade that is replacing the discipline-centered approach was in fact launched over a decade ago. Today's student-activist movement, according to its closest observers, began when SLATE was first organized at the University of California, Berkeley, and made its first set of "demands." [2] Its platform was announced to the university's academic community in the *Cal Reporter* in March 1958.

> We will be concerned with students as citizens in society—with their involvement with national and international issues.
>
> We will be concerned with education—with whether or not the University helps us to be open-minded, thinking individuals.
>
> We will be concerned with academic function and civil liberties. We ask only a fair hearing in the open marketplace of ideas. [3]

During the next six years these small sounds of dissent were to grow into an insistent voice of protest, until in October 1964 participants in the annual meeting of the American Council on Education, scheduled that year in San Francisco, read the *Chronicle*'s headline over breakfast—*Students Riot in Berkeley*—and were stunned. By the close of that academic year many administrative officers and faculty members had begun to wonder whether student unrest on the American

Dr. Axelrod is professor of world literature, San Francisco State College, and lecturer in higher education, University of California, Berkeley. The project described in this chapter was directed by Dr. Axelrod at the Center for Research and Development in Higher Education, Berkeley, where he served as visiting research specialist from 1967 to 1969.

1. James R. Squire, "The Running Water and the Standing Stone," p. 525.
2. Joseph Katz, *The Student Activists*. See also Joseph Axelrod et al., *Search for Relevance*, chapter 6; Richard Flacks, "Student Power and the New Left."
3. Quoted in Axelrod et al., *Search for Relevance*, p. 91.

campus should not be taken as a sign of curricular and instructional failure. The Danforth Foundation's *Annual Report for 1964–65* gave voice to those reflections. "Nearly every discussion of student unrest," the *Report* stated, "points out the relation of that problem to the poor teaching that is often found on college and university campuses." [4]

The Humanist's Response

For the professor in the humanities, more than for his colleagues in the social and natural sciences, the cry *Relevance!* has been a particularly difficult demand to respond to. Many humanists have answered in creative ways, but more often the reaction has been either to retreat or to freeze. The natural scientist can pretend the cry is not directed to him. As the nation stands on the threshold of the "technetronic" age, everything he does somehow automatically appears to be relevant to the future of mankind. The social scientist responds fairly easily by reorganizing his materials for a "problems" approach. [5] But the humanist is caught between the neutralism that his scholarship requires and the direct involvement in man's problems that the characteristic ideology of American humanism demands.

The situation of the humanist is made more difficult by several basic tenets of the student revolution that are identical with his own traditional stance. In the first place both the revolutionary and the humanist are antibureaucracy, indeed antiorganization in general. Both stress the worth and dignity of the human being as an individual. Both prize individual creative expression, and the humanist spends his life working on, and teaching, the greatest products of such expression. Second, both react against the application of logic and rationality to those areas of life that cannot, they believe, be governed by logic or rationality. The humanist has fought on almost every campus to preserve the legitimacy and academic acceptance of nonrationalistic modes of perception. For the same reason, he has battled against creeping scientism in the humanities. The student revolutionary takes the same attitude: "Don't send us questionnaires," he says to the behavioral scientist who wants to study student activism. "Just listen to our music!" [6]

4. Quoted in Lewis B. Mayhew, *Colleges Today and Tomorrow*, p. 163.

5. Many humanists have of course adopted the same solution. "Give Relevance half a chance and it will convert the Arts and Humanities into social sciences," a *New Republic* editor quips as he comments on the possible consequences of President Nixon's recommendation to Congress that the life of the Arts and Humanities Endowments be extended for three years and their funds doubled (*New Republic*, 3 January 1970, p. 9).

6. Based on a comment made by Frank Bardacke, graduate student at the University of California, Berkeley, in his presentation as a member of a symposium on The Persistent Student Voice in the Contemporary University at the annual meeting of the American Psychological Association, September 1968, San Francisco.

Third, although the humanist has fought overspecialization and professionalization in the liberal arts, he has capitulated more often than he would like to admit; many English departments are more highly professionalized than many schools of business. Still, the humanist's ideological stance on this point is unambiguous. The revolutionary student, voicing the same ideology, condemns the university for the ease with which it serves big business and the big professions and big science, producing for them, not men and leaders, but robots and "achiever" types; that is, nonindividuals whose college degrees signify their readiness to perform the exact tasks that industry demands.

Since the humanist has traditionally represented these principles, why should he retreat or freeze into paralysis at the cry *Relevance!* One reason might be that he misunderstands the message. There is no need for him to teach *King Lear* as *Endgame* if he does not agree with Jan Kott on this point; nor need he include Mao Tse-tung's delicate poems in his Introduction to World Literature course, especially if he feels uncomfortable with old-style Chinese verse. As for Bob Dylan, the humanist has no reason to include him in the Major Figures course unless he wants to, even if a University of California sociologist does see him as "a prophet and explicator of the future." [7]

Many humanists misunderstand the cry *Relevance!* Thinking it means merely modernity, the here-and-now, they are justifiably suspicious. "It does not make sense," as the vice-chairman of the English department at Berkeley said recently, "to propose a survey course in English literature *beginning* with T. S. Eliot!" [8]

In its deepest sense, relevance does not mean modernity. Those who would reform curricula according to the requirements of relevance argue their cause on quite different grounds. Their central opposition to standard curricula in humanistic studies revolves around two major principles on which all such curricula are built. The first of these asserts that a degree program in the discipline must cover the subject matter of the discipline systematically. According to this principle, the request made by many radical students—that they be allowed to study only those problems they find meaningful—must be rejected. The principle of self-determination violates the principle of systematic coverage of subject matter.

A second principle on which standard curricula are built asserts that a course cannot be offered on a given topic if no qualified faculty expert is available to conduct it. For example, a large West Coast

7. Jan Kott, *Shakespeare, Our Contemporary;* Kai-yu Hsu, *Twentieth-Century Chinese Poetry;* Ralph J. Gleason, "Bob Dylan."

8 At a meeting of the Higher Education Colloquy, February 1969, University of California, Berkeley.

English department has wished to offer a seminar in James Baldwin under its Major Figures course number, but it has not yet been able to find a qualified faculty member to give the seminar. The suggestion that the course be organized by a student or faculty member in the department was rejected. To accept this suggestion—that is, to allow a group of students and faculty to organize a course and use the university and community resources to teach it to themselves—was tantamount, the department felt, to throwing academic standards to the winds.

Many activist students and faculty supporters have offered against these two traditional principles arguments that have raised no small number of hackles. They point out, first of all, that systematic coverage of a field is an illusion. At best, there is only selective coverage of subject matter in a field; such coverage is more or less identical from one campus to the next only so long as arbitrary agreements remain in force among most of the faculty members in the field. For example, there is common agreement that the literature studied in an English department shall include a fairly standard sampling of non-English works (studied in English translation) and shall exclude almost every original work written in English outside of British and American literatures. Before World War II there was fairly common agreement on coverage, not only in literature but also in language and linguistics. These agreements, however, have begun to break down; the once-common subject matter of an English department is now taking different shapes on different campuses. Department X, following the traditional emphasis on literature, is even today only lightly involved with linguistic science; department Y has, however, more heavily moved into linguistics, and that new emphasis is reflected in the "coverage" required of its degree candidates. In department M, literary criticism and aesthetics have come to be central; in N, they are still mere appendages to literary history.

A pointed example is the controversy over the inclusion of the study of the film as an art form. At one time there was general agreement that while dramas were appropriate for study as literature, films were not. But today many faculty members look upon the film as the most expressive art form of the century and press for its inclusion among the subjects studied in literature departments.

There are good reasons then, the argument concludes, why the principle of systematic coverage as the basis for building a curriculum has come to be seriously questioned. Indeed, new principles for organizing curricula are being sought in many places.[9] Radical students

9. Axelrod et al., *Search for Relevance,* chapters 4 and 5; Joseph J. Schwab, *The College Curriculum and Student Protest.*

and their faculty supporters suggest the *fais ce que voudras* approach—
do what thou wilt. If a student happens to be interested in Joyce, he
simply starts with Joyce, not planning where he will move next. But
Joyce, he finds, inevitably leads to Homer; and so he must move to
Homer; and in Homer he finds new meaning as well as a key to Joyce.
If a student happens to be interested in Albee, he might wish to learn
whether Mrs. Woolf's name is used merely for the pun or whether
Albee's play really connects with something about her life and work;
to work at that problem, he must place her essays (especially the
feminist ones), a novel or two, and perhaps *Orlando* on his reading
list. If *Orlando,* then he is inevitably led to the despised English
literature survey, for he will surely want to discover what Orlando's
sexual transformation in that odd biography symbolizes. And so it
goes; a tutorial session with a culturally disadvantaged student may
lead, with the help of a resourceful instructor, to a systematic analysis
of a nonstandard American dialect.

The traditional faculty member listens to such suggestions with
some impatience and replies that the *fais ce que voudras* approach is
inappropriate for college students. It is appropriate, he argues, only
for mature learners who have sufficient knowledge to guide themselves
well and who have the inner discipline to persist in their intentions.
The path might also have been right for some gentleman of leisure in
the past century (indeed it apparently was for Virginia Woolf her-
self), but it is surely not institutionally feasible for the adolescent
today. Moreover, his reply continues, how can a student be permitted to
receive credit for pursuing an interest in, say, astrology or in the
practice of magic? Yet, if the principle of self-determination is carried
to its logical conclusion, a faculty member would not have the right to
say of *The Beard,* "That is not worth spending time on" or of *Charley's
Aunt,* "*That* is not even literature."

There is another objection the traditional faculty member poses.
When a group of students wish to study subject matter their instructor
knows nothing about, what is he to do? His training has prepared him
to teach them a Shakespearean sonnet, but they have decided they
would rather read some African poems in English translation. What
then?

The radical students and faculty reply that of course no instructor
should feel obliged to do something he does not wish to do or does not
feel qualified to do. But surely, if he has had special training in poetry,
and if he does not mind reading some African poetry, there is no
doubt he can be helpful to his students. It is evident he probably could
not do with it all that he was planning to do with the Shakespearean
sonnet, for he is no expert in African studies; but one might hope that

he *is* a more sophisticated student of poetry than the members of his class. The new approach based on the principle of relevance asks students and instructor to pursue the inquiry together, each making the contribution he can make. The basic requirement for every member of the group is sincerity, and the basic requirement for the faculty member specifically is that he should be a faster, more sophisticated learner than most of the students in the group.

Whatever the rhetoric that clothes this response of the radicals, it brings into focus an important point: relevance is no more inherently characteristic of one kind of subject matter than of another—a work of Mrs. Woolf's rather than one of Mme. de Stael's, a piece performed on the Moog synthesizer rather than on the viola da gamba, in Swahili rather than Sanskrit, the film *Rashomon* rather than Job. Relevance resides in the relationships between the student and the instructor as they jointly pursue inquiries upon whatever subject matter they touch.

A clearer way of stating this point is that today's students are not asking to *be taught*—they are asking to be given the freedom to *learn*. The difference between these is indicated by the difference in verb form. To be taught is the passive form; to learn, the active. That difference between passivity and activity in the educative process is crucial; it is like the difference between death and life.

FIVE TEACHING STYLES

As part of a project the author has been directing at the Center for Research and Development in Higher Education, University of California, he has attempted to explore the classroom styles of college teachers. He has been particularly interested in the implications of the principle of relevance for curricular-instructional reform.[10] Out of that study, there emerged a typology of teaching styles which posited the following five faculty prototypes:

A. The Drillmaster (or Recitation Class Teacher)
B. The Content-Centered Faculty Member
C. The Instructor-Centered Faculty Member
D. The Intellect-Centered Faculty Member
E. The Person-Centered Faculty Member

Types A and B are subject-matter–centered instructors. Types D and E are student-centered instructors. Type C, the type most common in the humanities, cannot be characterized as either subject-matter-centered or student-centered in his teaching style. These distinctions will become clear in the following descriptions illustrating the types.

---

10. An interim report appeared in 1968: "Curricular Change: A Model for Analysis," *Research Reporter,* 3, no. 3.

A. THE DRILLMASTER (OR RECITATION CLASS TEACHER)

Dr. A has the reputation of being one of the best foreign-language audiolingual instructors in the country. He often gives professional demonstrations at modern-language meetings, and visitors to such meetings find Dr. A's classes breathtaking. The tempo in drill work, for example, is subtly varied, regulated to the split second to serve best the precise purposes Dr. A has set.

In foreign-language teaching, drill sessions have played an indispensable role in programs that have adopted the audiolingual approach.[11] The foreign-language field is, however, not the only one in which the drillmaster style can be found. It is commonly used in many classes where students must acquire a skill that does not depend on reasoning or must learn a body of information by rote. The objective of such sessions is for the student to develop a semiautomatic response to particular kinds of cues. The instructor tries to help the student acquire the ability to respond immediately without having to think. If, therefore, he encourages his students to reason out their responses for each exercise, he is teaching against his objective. As a consequence, in the best sessions led by type-A instructors, the ratiocinative processes are kept at a minimum. The acquisition of a skill, or a body of information if that is the objective of the course, is attained by drill and repetition rather than by a problem-solving process; clearly, it is more economical to attain such knowledge through drill than through the time-consuming processes of discovery or inquiry. On the other hand, if the objective of a course is the acquisition of a skill or other knowledge that depends on reasoning or involves problem solving—for example, the ability to decide which pieces of data are relevant to a new problem in the field or the ability to draw generalizations from a new set of particulars—the drillmaster style is obviously not appropriate.

The Berkeley-project researchers observed many college classes where the drillmaster style was used with astonishing results—in elementary piano, second-semester Russian, introduction to logic, and remedial English. They also visited some classes in which this teaching style predominated but in which the acquisition of information was the primary objective—a course in Western civilization, a survey of

11. In programs that have not adopted the audiolingual approach, there is often considerable emphasis on learning the rules first and then "reasoning it out." But even among foreign language teachers for whom rigorous audiolingual drill is essential, there are sharp disagreements in both theory and practice. See Guillermo del Olmo, Dwight Bolinger, and Victor E. Hanzeli, "Professional and Pragmatic Perspectives on the Audiolingual Approach."

English literature, an art-history course, a study of the world's religions. In these classes, investigators observed students doing little besides reciting definitions, explanations, and generalizations they had memorized from one or more books or from the instructor's lectures.

In the drillmaster style, whether a skill or a body of information is being taught, the instructor is the ultimate authority, and the student has few choices open to him or demanded of him. There are no decisions for him to make; with few exceptions, there is only one acceptable response to each cue that is given him. This is the major difference between type A and the instructor types that remain to be discussed. Type B, type C, type D, and type E use discovery, inquiry, problem solving, discussion (as opposed to recitation in type-A classes), and regular or periodic formal lectures. These four faculty types thus have much in common. Each teaching style is nevertheless distinguishable in significant ways from each of the others. As the following pages show, Dr. B, Dr. C, Dr. D, and Dr. E each has his own view of the teaching-learning process, and each of these views demands a different kind of behavior from the instructor and from his students. Moreover, while each of these instructors, including also Dr. A, pursues excellence within his own framework, the criteria by which one kind of excellence may be compared with another depend largely upon one's philosophy of relevance.

B. THE CONTENT-CENTERED FACULTY MEMBER

Dr. B happens to be an art historian, but he is an excellent representative of the content-centered instructor type. In shoptalk with Dr. B, one is immediately struck by the fact that he does not find either his task or his discipline ambiguous. His task, he says, is to cover the materials of his discipline systematically in order to help his students master them. And he is quite clear on which subject matter ought to be covered, how topics are to be arranged, and what students in each of the courses offered by his department should achieve. He believes that courses carrying the same label on different campuses should cover the same general topics. A course labeled Classic and Early Christian Art or Modern Art, for example, ought to cover the same subject matter, whether it is given on his campus or on another. He has therefore resisted efforts in his department to introduce nonstandard ways of organizing the material of his field.

Just as Dr. B has a clear sense of his own role, that of teacher, so he has a clear sense of the student's role: the student is there to learn. Dr. B believes that the view sometimes put forward by students about the teaching-learning process—that it ought to consist of joint inquiry

—is nonsense. Occasionally, when joint inquiry appears to take place in Dr. B's class, it is in fact merely a pedagogic device by which he helps a student arrive at a solution to a prestructured problem. Dr. B thus places his emphasis on the student's mastery of the material that has already been discovered by workers in his field. In other words, his students are led to answers, or are given answers directly, that are already known and agreed upon by scholars like Dr. B. The notion that the professor can learn something during a class discussion with undergraduates appears utterly foreign to Dr. B's conception of teaching and learning.

There are two basic conceptions that underlie Dr. B's view of himself as a teacher and his activity in the classroom. When Dr. B envisions the ideal student, the perfect product of his efforts, a fairly static image emerges. More important, the image is identical for all students. It pictures someone who has perfectly mastered the subject matter that Dr. B has presented in the course and has assigned for out-of-class study. The second conception basic to Dr. B's view of the teaching-learning process is that the change taking place in the students in his classes is a more-or-less identical process for all the students. It is a movement from relative ignorance to relative knowledge. For example, when a student takes his Primitive Art course, which deals with the arts of Africa, Polynesia, and pre-Columbian America, Dr. B envisions students entering the course knowing next to nothing about the arts of those cultures and moving slowly, under his tutelage, from this state of ignorance to a state of knowledge.

Dr. B prefers an emotion-free atmosphere in his classroom. An aura of scholarly objectivity and noninvolvement surrounds his person; a cool, rational approach to problems characterizes his classroom as well as his person. His relationship to students, both in class and out, is cool and distant, although not unfriendly. And students are quick to sense that a private space, which they may not penetrate, encircles Dr. B wherever he goes.

Since Dr. B is also a department chairman, the interviewer asked him what he looks for when he recruits faculty members. "Oh," he replied, "the candidate's reputation in the field is of course the main thing. Or in a young man, promise and potential. Of course he should have certain other qualifications as well. He ought to be articulate and patient. And he should be capable of getting along well with colleagues."

Project visitors to Dr. B's classes did not find him the most exciting teacher they had ever seen, but they concluded that no student would find cause for complaint. The materials Dr. B deals with are intrinsically interesting, and he has the intelligence not to get in their way.

C. THE INSTRUCTOR-CENTERED FACULTY MEMBER

Dr. C is a professor of English literature and one of the most talked-about faculty members on his campus. He is a critic for one of the widely circulated national magazines, and his name is a household word among intellectuals.

The major role he plays in his classroom is that of a model, demonstrating to his students what he believes are the best ways of apprehending the works and handling the concepts of literature. For Dr. C it is not the subject matter of a field that ought to be at the center of class activity, but what an instructor does with that subject matter. Nor is it mastery of subject matter that his students are expected to work at as their primary goal. It is rather the ability to demonstrate in papers and examinations that they can imitate Dr. C's ways of conceiving of problems, defining them, formulating them, reasoning about them, and handling data pertinent to them. Like Dr. B, he sees teaching as mainly the transmission of knowledge, but there is nevertheless a difference. When Dr. B conceives of knowledge, he thinks of the fruits of knowledge; that is, he conceives of knowledge as a product. Dr. C sees knowledge as process.

The class time in Dr. C's courses is used entirely for two activities: lectures, which Dr. C characterizes as "a kind of demonstration," and question-and-answer periods, which he refers to as "discussion." The discussions do not generally involve extended dialog between instructor and students. Most often, students use the after-lecture discussion period to challenge Dr. C's approach or point of view. He obviously enjoys these challenges and encourages them, and as he is an excellent showman, he almost always emerges victorious.

Dr. C is interested in the teaching process, has a coherent conception of his role as teacher, plays a completely central role in the class, prepares for that role with great diligence, and obviously enjoys being in the limelight. He gives the impression of authority and independence that attracts students—he has, indeed, charisma—and he takes seriously the education of undergraduates. During out-of-class discussions with students, Dr. C responds warmly, especially to those who show warmth for him. He has rapport with many students, even though all conversation with them begins with him and his ideas and, sooner or later, moves back to him and his ideas.

Like Dr. B, Dr. C is generally satisfied with the standard grading-system. He uses a single grading-criterion: the exactitude with which students demonstrate in examination exercises that they can imitate his approaches, perspectives, conceptions, and formulations or, alternatively, the degree to which they imitate figures whom Dr. C admires. Such figures include critics of literature whose work Dr. C recommends. Dr. C impressed project investigators as a unique personality with ideas about which he feels passionately and which he expresses with verve, originality, great seriousness, and infectious humor.

The difference between the type-B and type-C faculty member is exactly the difference Daniel Bell draws between a scholar and an intellectual. A scholar, he says, "has a bounded field of knowledge, a tradition, and seeks to find a place in it, adding to the accumulated, tested knowledge of the past as to a mosaic." The intellectual, on the other hand, "begins with *his* experience, *his* individual perceptions of the world, *his* privileges and deprivations, and judges the world by these sensibilities." [12] That distinction states the most significant difference about the teaching styles of these two types. The best type-B class sessions, even when they are conducted by rather different instructors, look very much the same. The instructors keep out of the way of their materials and carry on their classroom work in similar fashion. The project investigators found that a session with one type-B instructor on a given topic was very much like a session devoted to the same topic conducted by a type-B colleague of his. They found the reverse true of type-C instructors; each had a different perspective, and a class session with a type-C instructor was never similar to another instructor's class session on the same topic.

Dr. C's teaching philosophy goes hand in hand with his belief that in each department there ought to be a diversity of teacher models. Among his departmental colleagues in English literature, for example, several represent schools of criticism completely different from his own; and a few do not engage in literary criticism per se, being of that generation when the literary scholar was trained to engage in value-free historical research. Since no single faculty member could serve as the model for the several major styles of inquiry in the field of literature, Dr. C believes the undergraduate should be subjected to a variety of faculty models. In this way, the faculty do not reinforce one another's biases; and, while their modes of treatment may present a welter of diversity to the student, he will at least emerge from the experience realizing that no single perspective or single mode of inquiry is universally accepted in the field as the right road.

Many faculty members in humanistic studies wonder, however, whether such diversity is educationally sound. Among them, a number hold the view that the undergraduate ought to be presented with a single esthetic and critical framework—any respectable one will do—and ought to work at it in sufficient depth, rigor, and inten-

12. Daniel Bell, *The End of Ideology*, pp. 372 ff.

sity to enable him to master it and use it with ease. Dr. D holds this view. Indeed, this philosophic difference between Dr. C and Dr. D accounts in large part for their great differences in teaching style.

D. THE INTELLECT-CENTERED FACULTY MEMBER

Dr. D believes in training of a particularly rigorous intellectual sort. Because he is in a department where the faculty represent a wide variety of perspectives and modes of inquiry, Dr. D finds that, with the exception of a few disciples, he does not have students long enough under his tutelage to be able to carry his program of training through to a satisfactory conclusion. He is, however, highly successful with those students who become his disciples and, fortunately for his state of morale, even this limited success is a source of great satisfaction to him.

Like Dr. C, Dr. D distinguishes sharply between knowledge as product and knowledge as process. As a member of an interdisciplinary department of humanities, he condemns the courses in his department that derive from the conception of knowledge as product. He believes the focus of class activity should be shifted. The teaching-learning process must not limit itself to a study of the products of rational activity; it should concentrate on rational activity itself. In Dr. D's courses the emphasis is on the how and why of knowledge, rather than the what.

Dr. D was asked whether, for his point of view to be effective, it did not have to be adopted by the other faculty members within his own department. "That's the difficulty," he replied. "Not merely in my own department. To be really effective, it must be adopted by the whole college!"

Since type-D instructors are primarily concerned with the intellectual development of students, analysis and problem solving constitute their basic teaching means and the major devices they use in testing students. Whether a type-D faculty member teaches a traditionally academic subject—for example, literary history or criticism, philosophy, art or music history or criticism, history of ideas—or a subject in the performing and creative arts—for example, creative writing, drama, dance, plastic arts, music—his emphasis remains intellectual. He characteristically does not concern himself with detailed coverage of the field but concentrates on one or several modes of analysis, teaching students how to approach and apprehend artworks rather than transmitting a body of knowledge about them. Often his examination consists of presenting to students one or more new works, never discussed in the class sessions, to which students apply the same modes of analysis that he and the class have worked through together.

E. THE PERSON-CENTERED FACULTY MEMBER

Dr. E shares much in common with Dr. D, for both are student-centered faculty members. But he believes that Dr. D's emphasis on intellectual development and on rational activity can only, in the long run, prove destructive to the student or be, at best, ineffective. Dr. E does not believe that intellectual development ought to be split off from other aspects of the human personality; moreover, if an instructor succeeds in effecting such a split, Dr. E believes such an instructor does the learner harm.

In spite of this major difference between them, Dr. D and Dr. E share a fundamental assumption. Both believe that a philosophy of teaching must be undergirded by a theory of human development, that is, a theory of how men achieve their fullest powers of humanness. Dr. D believes that one can keep, and ought to keep, the two developmental cycles separate: progress in academic matters on the one hand and progress in nonacademic problems (problems of identity and of intimacy) on the other. Dr. E insists that these two cycles must be maintained in a dynamic relationship, each supporting the other. If this is so, Dr. E argues, then both growth cycles become the concern of the college teacher; and if the college teacher is not qualified or not willing to deal with the nonacademic cycle, then the whole growth process as the college student moves into adulthood is placed in jeopardy. The choice open to college teachers is clear, Dr. E asserts; if they do not wish to concern themselves with the development of the student as a person, then they must be content to play no significant part at all in his education. Since most college faculty members do not wish—or are not qualified—to work with the student as a person, it is not surprising, Dr. E points out, that according to the research evidence, faculty members have not had a significant impact on the development of college students.[13]

Since he does not hesitate to voice this point of view publicly, Dr. E is not popular among many of his colleagues. Nor are they, by any means, silent. When he charges them with mistaking a set of ceremonial acts for an educational process, they accuse him of lowering academic standards. The likelihood is that Dr. E would be quite uncomfortable, since the faculty climate on his campus supports his more conservative colleagues, were it not for the fact that his field is dramatic arts. Moreover, his department, widely known for the high calibre of its work, is responsible primarily for courses on the performance level, having made an agreement about ten years ago with

---

13. Evidence accumulated over the last forty years is presented in Kenneth A. Feldman and Theodore M. Newcomb, *The Impacts of College on Students*.

the English faculty that the traditional courses in the history and criticism of dramatic literature would be offered by the English department.

Though he has no formal training in psychology, Dr. E is conversant with recent personality theory. He seems to know the work of Erik Erikson and Nevitt Sanford. During interviews he stressed his conception of what a student does when he "learns" something. His comments on this point can be summarized as follows: A student does not learn unless he is challenged. A challenge is not simply a matter of proper motivation but is related to the task. A challenging task not only elicits from the student a desire to do it but also demands that he use resources and strategies he has not used in doing other tasks. When a student is given an assignment that he can manage with his existing repertoire of responses, he will use only that repertoire. There is no challenge in such an assignment, nor is there any growth. But if the student is faced with a situation he cannot manage with his existing repertoire of responses, he must invent or find new ones. If these work, they are integrated with the rest of his personality.

According to Dr. E's analysis, there is little challenge in most assignments students receive in their college courses. Freshmen enter college, for example, having learned in previous school experiences how to memorize facts presented by others and generalizations formulated by others. Many college courses require them to memorize still more facts and principles. Since they already possess a way of organizing experience to meet such demands, there is no need for them to seek a more complex way to fulfill these assignments. In this way, the "educational" process may actually do harm. If the student discovers that his existing behavioral structure is adequate to meet the demands put upon it by the assignments his instructors give him, he tends to resist any other pressures to expand that structure. Thus, instead of joining noncurricular campus forces that urge the student to expand, to develop new resources, and to discover himself and the world, his academic experiences may function in just the opposite way.

THIRTEEN KEY QUESTIONS

Similarities and differences between and among these five teaching styles may be seen more easily if one attempts to answer, for each of them, these thirteen questions.

1. When the faculty member draws a fairly concrete mental picture of the ideal "product" emerging from his courses—that is, students who complete the courses and undergo precisely the changes the instructor had hoped for—is the image identical for all students?

2. When the faculty member conceives of the changes he wishes to

effect in students—the kinds of changes, the direction of change, and the like—does he imagine that those students who reach the goals he has set for them have changed in basically the same way?

3. Does class activity concern itself almost exclusively with cognitive knowledge? Or does class activity also reflect significant attention to knowledge that is in the affective domain?

4. In his efforts to help students acquire knowledge, does the instructor mainly transmit the fruits of knowledge? Does he see knowledge primarily as product, or does he also see knowledge as process?

5. Are the activity carried on in class and the activity students perform to prepare for the class session and for examinations almost always of a rational nature, characterized by the formulation of concepts and explanations and by reasoning, generalizing, and particularizing? Or is there significant attention given to the irrational and the nonrational?

6. Are decisions about the selection and sequence of topics and the organization of class sessions made solely by the instructor? Or does he seek advice from his students during the course of the class session or give responsibility to the group for any of these decisions?

7. Is the instructor particularly and explicitly concerned with communication between each student and his classmates?

8. Do lectures by the instructor or by guests, or lecture-like presentations such as educational films, play a significant role in the class sessions?

9. In a student-instructor dialog during discussions and question-and-answer periods, is the student often an initiator? Or does the instructor almost always initiate the dialog by asking a question, requesting a reaction, or setting a problem?

10. Does the instructor often model the learning process or the process of discovery?

11. Does the instructor use the pressures felt by the student group, and opinions expressed by it, to motivate individuals in it?

12. Are cooperative projects, involving two or more students, often undertaken as an integral part of the work to be done for the course?

13. Is the faculty member generally satisfied with the standard testing and grading system?

For four of these questions (1, 3, 5, and 12), Dr. B, Dr. C, and Dr. D basically agree, while Dr. E stands alone in his response. For four others (2, 4, 9, and 10) Dr. C, Dr. D, and Dr. E agree, while Dr. B stands alone in his response. Of the five remaining questions (6, 7, 8, 11, and 13) Dr. B and Dr. C are in agreement, while Dr. D and Dr. E disagree with the other two but basically agree with one another. Since Dr. A's classes are not characterized by inquiry or by problem solving, a large number of these questions do not apply; for those that do, Dr. A's answers are identical with Dr. B's.[14]

WHO IS THE BEST TEACHER?

Is one of the five teaching styles better for humanistic studies than the others? The answer is that the prototypes described here are neither good nor bad in themselves. Within each of the styles, it is possible to find excellent teachers and poor teachers. Thus each style has its own excellence, and the problem facing the young instructor entering the field is not an easy one. How is he to judge whether one or another kind of excellence is the one he should pursue? His basic criterion must arise out of his definition of relevance.

As an example, if he were to accept the *fais ce que voudras* philosophy presented earlier in this chapter, it is evident that Dr. E's style is the only one of the five that fits that particular definition of relevance. It is also evident, however, that not every young instructor in humanistic studies (even those under 30!) would choose to organize the teaching-learning process around encounter and involvement or insist that it is the instructor's duty to encourage in students a sense of commitment.

Nonetheless, whether the problem of relevance is faced in that way or in some other way, it must be directly faced. A devoted teacher cannot do otherwise. "Only in the humanities," William C. DeVane has observed, "does the old ideal of the productive scholar who is at the same time a devoted classroom teacher still flourish." [15] On one point, surely, there is universal agreement among humanists in the academic world: humanities faculties must seek the wisdom and strength necessary to maintain that old ideal in the grim years ahead.

14. A detailed analysis of the responses to the thirteen questions is given in the final report of the Berkeley project, *Model Building for Undergraduate Colleges,* available through ERIC.
15. William C. DeVane, "The College of Liberal Arts," p. 7.

Bibliographical Essay

There is almost universal agreement that the most important book of the sixties in the field of higher education is the monumental collection of essays compiled by Nevitt Sanford under the title *The American College* (New York: John Wiley & Sons, 1962), which is now available in paperback. For graduate studies, the most stimulating book since 1960 is Oliver C. Carmichael's *Graduate Education: A Critique and a Program* (New York: Harper & Row, Publishers, 1961), but a forthcoming book by Ann Heiss is eagerly anticipated by the profession. The latest book by Algo Henderson, tentatively entitled *The Innovative Spirit*, is also due to appear in fall 1970. The annual volumes edited by G. Kerry Smith under the title *Current Issues in Higher Education* contain important essays; the latest of these—*Stress and Campus Response: Current Issues in Higher Education, 1968* (San Francisco: Jossey-Bass, 1968) and *Agony and Promise: Current Issues in Higher Education, 1969* (San Francisco: Jossey-Bass, 1969)—contain illuminating essays on curricular and instructional problems.

For humanistic studies, a superb collection of essays was gathered together by Arthur A. Cohen to honor Robert M. Hutchins: *Humanistic Education and Western Civilization* (New York: Holt, Rinehart & Winston, 1964). As for the individual disciplines, there is an enormous literature on curricular and instructional problems, but much of it is at the folklore and anecdotal level. One wishes there were more volumes of the calibre of *The College Teaching of English*, edited by John C. Gerber, John H. Fisher, and Curt A. Zimansky (New York: Appleton-Century-Crofts, 1965).

Recent volumes in the Jossey-Bass Series in Higher Education of interest to the humanist are Paul Heist, ed., *The Creative College Student: An Unmet Challenge* (1968); L. E. Dennis and Renate Jacob, eds., *The Arts in Higher Education* (1968); Joseph Axelrod, Mervin B. Freedman, Winslow R. Hatch, Joseph Katz, and Nevitt Sanford, *Search for Relevance: Campus in Crisis* (1969); and Philip Runkel, Roger Harnson, and Margaret Runkel, *The Changing College Classroom* (1969). A new book by Joseph Axelrod, tentatively titled *The Liberated University*, is now in preparation. These volumes are published by Jossey-Bass, San Francisco.

Works Cited

Axelrod, Joseph; Freedman, Mervin B.; Hatch, Winslow R.; Katz, Joseph; and Sanford, Nevitt. *Search for Relevance.* San Francisco: Jossey-Bass, 1969.

Bell, Daniel. *The End of Ideology.* Glencoe, Ill.: Free Press, 1960.

del Olmo, Guillermo; Bolinger, Dwight; and Hanzeli, Victor E. "Professional and Pragmatic Perspectives on the Audiolingual Approach." *Foreign Language Annals* 2, no. 1 (October 1968) : 19-50.

DeVane, William C. "The College of Liberal Arts." In *The Contemporary University: U. S. A.,* edited by Robert S. Morison. Boston: Beacon Press, 1966.

Feldman, Kenneth A., and Newcomb, Theodore M. *The Impacts of College on Students.* San Francisco: Jossey-Bass, 1969.

Flacks, Richard. "Student Power and the New Left." Paper read at American Psychological Association annual meeting, September 1969.

Gleason, Ralph J. "Bob Dylan: Poet to a Generation." *This World, San Francisco Chronicle* magazine section, 18 August 1968.

Hsu, Kai-yu. *Twentieth-Century Chinese Poetry.* Garden City, N.Y.: Doubleday & Co., 1963.

Katz, Joseph. *The Student Activists: Rights, Needs, and Powers of Undergraduates.* New Dimensions in Higher Education series. Washington: U. S. Department of Health, Education, and Welfare, 1967.

Kott, Jan. *Shakespeare, Our Contemporary.* New York: Doubleday & Co., Anchor Books, 1964.

Mayhew, Lewis B. *Colleges Today and Tomorrow.* San Francisco: Jossey-Bass, 1969.

Schwab, Joseph J. *The College Curriculum and Student Protest.* Chicago: University of Chicago Press, 1969.

Squire, James R. "The Running Water and the Standing Stone." *PMLA,* June 1968, pp. 523-29.

Teaching the Humanities

O. B. HARDISON, JR.

Any sane man asked to comment on the art of teaching will begin with a sense of humility bordering on the abject. Teaching is a creative activity, something that is largely made up as it goes, and until there is a satisfactory explanation of creativity itself, the basis of successful teaching will remain mysterious. It is not that rules and theories are lacking. From ancient times to the beginnings of the modern educational revolution with Rousseau and Pestalozzi, the twelve books of Quintilian's *Institute of Oratory* supplied pedagogues with a nearly crushing burden of rules and theories (most of them very sensible). Since then, theories have multiplied, very nearly in the geometric pattern of cells dividing in an ideal culture medium or of neutrons in the chain reaction that precedes an atomic explosion.

Alas, the new theories have not settled much of anything. They have made life more interesting for educational philosophers, but they have left the teacher stranded on that darkling plain where ignorant (and usually fanatical) armies clash by night. Each new theory comes equipped with its opinion polls to show that teachers by and large have no notion of what they are doing, with its touching examples of gleams of light in the prevailing gloom, and with its promises, propped up by masses of statistics, that the method proposed by its author is the ready and easy way to salvation, if only the sinister forces of tradition, habit, conformity, prejudice, vested interest, establishmentarianism, and the like can be destroyed.

The trouble is that a teacher can follow all the rules and still fall flat on his face. Poetry has been defined as what gets left out of the translation of a poem. If so, teaching may be what eludes the statistics and theories of the professors of education. Most people would probably agree that a good teacher needs knowledge of his subject, intelligence, tact, and kindness. The first of those desiderata, knowledge, is the only one that a teacher can do much about; it is also the one that is most often questioned. The rulebook has not been formulated that can teach anybody to be intelligent or tactful or kind. It never will

---

Dr. Hardison, at the time this paper was written, was professor of English literature, University of North Carolina. He is now director, Folger Shakespeare Library, Washington, D.C.

be, because these are qualities that show themselves only in specific situations. Tact demands that the teacher treat one student's poor performance with sympathy and another's with severity. It is generally kinder in the long run to allow students to accept full responsibility for what they do, but any teacher or administrator knows that there are innumerable cases where it is better to bend the rules than apply them rigorously. A good student who writes a careless paper has earned a failing grade, and his teacher does him no favor to let him think he has done well; a poor student who has done the best he can probably needs encouragement more than criticism. The point is that no action of the teacher can be judged in the abstract. One could almost say that the better the teacher, the more clearly his actions reflect this fact. The social sciences have yet to produce their Ptolemy, much less their Isaac Newton. Pending this event, the teacher is best advised to go modestly about his business, relying mostly on his developing sense of what works.

The point seldom made by educational theorists is that teaching is a cooperative affair. This is especially true of college teaching where the make-up of a class varies according to the level of the course, the fluctuating interests of students (one year T. S. Eliot is "in" and the next he may be "out"), and even the time and place the course is scheduled. It is also very likely true that teaching tends to be more cooperative in the humanities than in the sciences. The humanities teacher is usually talking about an experience that he has shared (or hopes he has shared) with his students. While the best teaching in the sciences may tend in this direction, the general emphasis in undergraduate science courses seems to be on moving a body of information along a one-way street from the head of the teacher to the head of the student.

If it is true that teaching in the humanities is cooperative, the teacher cannot assume full responsibility for the degree to which his course is "successful." He needs to be there to light the fire, but the materials have to be flammable in the first place, and the nature of the materials will determine whether the fire is hot and clear or smoulders away, generating more smoke than light. An actor should be infinitely adaptable. He should always play to his audience. But it is an old axiom in the theater that great drama demands great audiences. In the same way, anyone who has done much teaching knows that his sense of accomplishment—the exhilarating sense of having communicated attitudes and enthusiasms as well as the daily quota of information—varies greatly from class to class and even from period to period in the same class.

THE PROBLEM OF "GREAT" TEACHING

This is important because many young people entering college teaching today have an almost religious devotion to the ideal of "great teaching." The discovery that the teacher does not fully control the classroom—that a class is a *tertium quid* created by the participants—ought to be as exciting as the physics student's discovery that pulsars defy all current attempts at explanation, but often it is simply another disillusionment. Every young teacher wants to be admired by his students, singled out for praise in their course-evaluation booklets, and crowned with laurels by his dean during the award ceremonies at commencement. If he cannot achieve these goals entirely on his own, this must mean that "greatness" is a matter of luck—or, as he may begin to suspect over his second highball, a matter of being with the right people.

I, frankly, do not know what greatness is when applied to teaching. Normally the epithet *great* is reserved by historians for men who, by virtue of some accomplishment, usually violent and mostly with disastrous consequences for mankind at large, cannot be omitted from the undergraduate history textbooks. At the very least the historian usually waits a decent interval after his man's interment before calling him great. As applied to teaching, on the other hand, greatness is an instantaneous judgment. Public commendation can be deferred to the funeral, but swift promotion and extra pay are meaningful to the great teacher only while he is alive.

Who recognizes greatness—and how? Those who labor patiently in the vineyards, who speak not with the tongues of men and of angels, are inclined to the theory that teaching is largely patient, persistent attention to detail and that greatness should be measured by results. Unfortunately, teaching is not like basketweaving. No course ends with a neat, well-made basket. The results of teaching may take years to show themselves, or they may never be measurable at all. Everyone has a story about a teacher he disliked intensely but whose influence proved both permanent and beneficial. I myself once knew a teacher who by all current standards would be considered a total failure. He permitted no class participation, he skirted the edge of incoherence when he lectured, he was given to taking up large chunks of class time by reading bibliographies, and, so far as I know, he was innocent of seminal ideas. Yet there was a peculiar intensity and authority about the man that drove his students to heroic efforts when they were not being driven mad. Today, years after his death, many of his students are recognized as distinguished scholars and highly successful teachers. In some way his influence remains a living force, while the influence of a hundred more-polished, more-amiable teachers who were his contemporaries has disappeared. He could never have won an award for great (or, perhaps, even for mediocre) teaching while alive, but if success is best measured by results, he was undeniably a great teacher.

More than likely the historical judgment, as measured by results, is the valid one. The corollary is that preoccupation with "greatness" can be harmful to teachers, courses, and the humanities generally. The teacher must do his job partly on faith.

THE DEMAND FOR RELEVANCE

A second point of view is far more popular than the historical just now. It is common among students and beginning teachers, and it is intensified by the cold war between the generations. Students tend to judge teaching by its "relevance," by which they often mean entertainment. Should they read Plato? Not if he cannot be made relevant, the reply goes. Evidently, they are not to read Plato to enlarge their minds through the experience of his but to skim through his dialogs— or the excerpts in our anthologies—to find a few sentences here and there that can be salvaged for use in the latest confrontation. Since the young teacher tends to evaluate his success—his greatness—on the basis of his popularity, he frequently not only endorses this point of view but propagates it. The results are evident in two ways: first in the increasing emphasis of the humanities curriculum on the present at the expense of the past, and second in the popularity of course evaluations. That isolation in the present can be as damaging to a culture as isolation from other men can be to an individual is an unfashionable and hence an irrelevant truth, but a truth, nonetheless. That evaluations are essentially popularity polls disturbs only the unpopular. For the winners the conclusion that justice has been done, talent rewarded, virtue vindicated is inescapable.

Teachers can take comfort, perhaps, in the reflection that, although the debate is being carried on in new terms, its substance is as ancient as the debate that Plato mentioned between the poets and the philosophers. It is a debate essentially between educational conservatives and educational liberals, and when one sees it in this way the truths on both sides are obvious. The past *is* important, but this does not mean that classes should be dull. The pursuit of knowledge and beauty for their own sake is a precious human right, but many persons are lured into the appreciation of a Platonic dialog or a play by Shakespeare or a painting by Raphael by a projection, a special feature, that happens to touch their own immediate interests. The notion that, whatever greatness is, the teacher should strive for it will continue to influence students, administrators, the general public, and, most important, the teacher himself. The best course for the beginning teacher is to accept greatness if it is thrust upon him but not to worry too much if he seems to be heading for "mere competence" rather than greatness. After all, mere competence is not so commonplace that educators and laymen can afford to treat it with scorn.

To recognize that teaching is creative, that it is a cooperative venture, and that "greatness" has to be taken with a grain of salt is to make the first accommodations that all teachers must eventually make to an imperfect world. It is, basically, to recognize the limitations within which all men, but especially teachers, must work. If it produces a certain humility, it also gives the teacher some protection against the fads and claims of the educationists. This point leads me from the discussion of general principles to the present state of the art.

EXPERIMENTATION AND INNOVATION

The new teacher will find that he is entering the profession at a time of almost obsessive experimentation. Industry has contributed to this situation in ways that are not always particularly admirable, and it will increasingly do so in the future. Educational equipment is highly profitable. Its manufacturers grind out reams of optimistic publicity to convince the innocent that it is capable of solving age-old educational problems. Such equipment now includes program texts in book or book-plus-machine form, machines to teach rapid reading, audiovisual equipment, filmstrips, closed-circuit television installations, and computer-controlled devices ranging from equipment for grading papers to teaching machines. Medical advertisements are strictly controlled by federal legislation, but there is apparently no regulation of the printed and word-of-mouth publicity for teaching equipment. Yet such equipment is already playing a very large part in higher education. Junior colleges and small, backward liberal arts colleges are very likely most susceptible because their teachers are generally less sophisticated, less able to resist the advertisers' claims, and feel more guilty about their own limitations than do teachers at larger institutions. But the larger institutions are by no means immune to exaggerated claims, naive or rigged statistics, the eloquence of the company representative, and, above all, the economic argument that machines save manpower. And, of course, not all of the claims are false, and many are not consciously false.

The point is that educational gadgetry profoundly affects education. If, for example, a teacher has a machine for grading papers, he tends to increase class size, eliminate term papers, and give factual rather than essay examinations. The pressure is always there. It is easy to go further but almost impossible to go back. For better or for worse, the teacher will find himself under considerable pressure to use some gadgetry and to justify its use in the name of creative experimentation. It is to be hoped that the humanities can hold out more successfully than other fields against the gadgets, but the truth is that much of the gadgetry is consciously intended for market in the humanities.

Again, higher education has traditionally been suspicious of educational theorists, who have, in turn, concentrated most of their efforts on secondary education. Widespread criticism of college teaching has changed all this. Students are keenly aware from their first days in graduate school that teaching will be their major, if not their only, career responsibility. Most graduate departments now provide informal instruction in the art of college teaching, and courses with credit are becoming common. Meanwhile, encouraged by federal and foundation grants, educational theorists are rapidly increasing the bibliography of studies of college teaching. It is fashionable to base these studies on polls, and since the polls are often designed on the assumption that there is something drastically wrong with our methods of college teaching, it is perhaps not surprising that the results tend to confirm the assumption. One such poll that reached me about a year ago was supposed to collect information on the attitude of Ph.D.'s toward their graduate training. It was so completely dominated by the notion that the respondents would want to criticize that I found the only part I could fill out was the part asking for academic rank and years of service. I finally had to give up trying to answer and simply wrote a note to the originator of the poll saying that I was acutely embarrassed to have to admit that I enjoyed my graduate work, admired my teachers from a distance that we found mutually gratifying, and felt the requirements were quite reasonable.

Whatever the originator may have thought of this pathetic display of conformity, I am sure that he did not allow it to affect his results. At any rate, I cite the example merely to illustrate the quandary in which the teacher is likely to find himself today. He has been trained to work in certain well-defined ways, and he is now being told that he is archaic, fails to make use of current educational theory, ignores student interests, and generally subordinates teaching to research, which is assumed to be mostly irrelevant to his success in the classroom.

Finally, the teacher will find his problems complicated further by pressure to experiment whether he wants to or not. Like gadgets, educational experiments threaten to become an end in themselves. These range the gamut from full-scale curricula offered in free universities to interdisciplinary courses, special honors curricula, undergraduate seminars, years abroad, team teaching, independent readings, area studies, credit for off-campus jobs, and the like. The experimentation is reflected in the almost compulsive revisions and re-revisions of the humanities curriculum by both departments and university-wide committees.

While this is a heady situation and many of the experiments are fun, if not demonstrably superior to what they replace, there are obvious dangers. To what degree is the humanities curriculum being formed, not by the faculty, but by business interests, educationists, and students? To what degree should graduate schools open themselves to courses in the theory and methods of college teaching? Do such courses mean reducing or abandoning the traditional graduate-school emphasis on subject matter? Has the performance of the educationists at the secondary level been such as to warrant confidence in their ability to reform college education? And finally, at what point in the process of experimentation and course revision does the humanities curriculum cease to exist as a coherent, meaningful body of work and become simply a collection of courses to be taken in any order or combination?

The young teacher cannot escape these questions. Whether he faces them squarely or simply drifts along with whatever happens to be the current fashion, he will be involved in them more deeply than his elders, more deeply, perhaps, than any of his predecessors since the Renaissance. It is always possible, of course, that the questions are pseudoquestions. The humanities curriculum may reflect such deep internal imperatives that the current period of experimentation will prove to be just that—a period of experimentation after which things will settle back pretty much to their old norm. This may happen at institutions where the humanities continue to be important, while at the others experimentation will weaken an already shaky position and result ultimately in reversion to type—that is, reversion to an old-style polytechnic curriculum broadened to include the social sciences. But no one can be sure. The one thing the young teacher can be sure of is that, in addition to having to come to terms with the mysteries of teaching, he will, in the course of his career, have every one of his most cherished assumptions challenged. Whether he stands for tradition or change, he will have to justify himself before his students in the classroom and before his colleagues in his department and on interdepartmental committees.

WHAT GOALS FOR HUMANISTIC EDUCATION?

Thus far this discussion has concentrated on subjects that are to a degree the concern of every college teacher. They are, however, probably more important to the humanist than to the scientist. In theory, at least, the sciences have an objectivity, a definition that the humanities lack. Presumably, an engineering student has to take calculus. As long as the calculus teacher conveys the essential techniques, it is not crucial whether he is stimulating or boring, great or merely adequate. But what are students in general required to take in the humanities? A sampling of college catalogs shows that answers range from "nothing at all" to "great books" to "English Lit. Survey" to "x number of elective courses in any department classified under Humanities." In other words, the calculus teacher does not have to face the general questions (this does not mean he should ignore them), but the teacher of literature or music or art must face them.

In a sense most of the specific questions that arise in the teaching of literature, to take a single example, are corollaries of the general ones. They can, however, be considered in themselves, for they are as clearly reflected in cleavages among schools of literary critics as they are in national debates on the future of American education. The chronological, nationally oriented curricula that still underlie the programs of most departments of modern languages are the products of historical scholarship, the prevailing school in the late nineteenth century when the older departments were formed. Contrary to repeated assertions of its demise, historical criticism still flourishes. It assumes that the study of literature requires a student to assimilate a great deal of information that he will ultimately need for understanding (appreciation is desirable but not essential) literary works. American Studies is the latest and most vigorous offshoot of the historical point of view, in spite of the fact that most American Studies programs are billed as "experimental"—any port, I suppose, in a storm.

At its best the historical ideal involves the love of knowledge for its own sake. It collides head-on with the view that humanistic education should be a form of practical education—education for action. This idea is the one held, apparently, by most ancient and Renaissance educators. In its crudest form it underlies such masterpieces of the textbook writer's art as *Aesop's Fables* and *McGuffey's Reader*. A much more sophisticated form appears in the writing of Matthew Arnold and, in this country, Irving Babbitt. Both Arnold and Babbitt consider the humanities, literature in particular, vehicles of human value. The good teacher is more concerned with the values than the works in which they are contained, just as the housewife is presumably more interested in the soup than the can (this is not to deny the importance of packaging). In fact, the teacher tends to choose the works because they reflect certain values rather than because of their literary excellence. The function of the teacher is to make sure that the students recognize the values and, as far as possible, ingest them. As a corollary, the practical critic is much more likely to be interested in his students as persons than is the historical scholar. Ideally, the values should be passed on to the students in small discussion groups.

While the idea that the humanities are repositories of ethical and social value has its attractions, it does not treat humanistic learning as disinterested. And, of course, the values conveyed to the students tend to vary with the person conveying them. The values of Arnold and Babbitt were conservative. Both men regarded literature as a kind of substitute for religion, and both wished to use it to create an elite group—an establishment—that could protect society against the excesses of egalitarian democracy. In the thirties the Communist Party used the same arguments to justify indoctrination through literature in Marxist values. Today, the New Left regards literature as a weapon in the struggle against established values in general. One hears the argument that the basic "value" of art or literature is revolution. To the true believer, the artist is fundamentally radical, and his art is engaged. The teacher should cooperate with him by making this truth not only evident but attractive to students. Disinterestedness, the argument runs, is a disguise for escapism. Objectivity is a mirage; to attempt it is to confess moral cowardice.

The aesthetic position, which underlies, for example, much of the New Criticism, treats literature (and art in general) as valuable in itself. In their respect for an activity pursued for its own sake, the apologists of aestheticism are allied to the historical critics, but they are bitterly opposed to the idea that literature is an object of quantitative knowledge rather than an imaginative (and pleasurable) experience. The quest for knowledge—for facts—they argue, often becomes an obstacle to aesthetic appreciation rather than an aid. Students, they complain, spend more time reading *about* Shakespeare, Goethe, or Proust than reading the works themselves, with the result that literary study becomes a sterile scrambling after information.

Aesthetic critics oppose the Arnoldian theory of literature as value on different but equally emphatic grounds. While they agree that art is a repository of value, they argue that the value is aesthetic, not ethical or social. From their point of view, to use a work—say, *Oedipus* —as a means of teaching the need for an "inner check" or another work—say, *War and Peace*—as a representation of the relation between capitalism and war is to substitute moral or economic platitudes for enlarging personal experiences. To omit *Oedipus* from the curriculum to make room for a more "relevant" work—say, *Native Son*—is even worse. It is to deprive students of the chance to share in one of the major achievements of the imagination of Western man. From this point of view, the curriculum in which works are chosen for relevance rather than excellence guarantees cultural deprivation. Humanistic education should enrich the individual. It should contribute to his freedom, not condition him.

The young teacher will find that, give and take variations in vocabulary, these three positions remain fundamental in theories of education, studies of the teacher's role, systems of criticism, and designs for humanities curricula. More than likely most teachers end up espousing one thing in theory but groping ahead pragmatically when in the classroom. Judging from the number and loudness of voices raised in its support, the second position—the idea that the humanities are repositories of ethical and social value—is currently in the ascendant. Outside of the university the favored value-system is conservative and ethical, while within the favored system is radical and political. This situation has already led to embittered confrontations between legislatures and college faculties and between students and administrators. Whether the confrontations will continue and whether they will ultimately harm or benefit humanistic education is anybody's guess. Even if they are harmful, the argument can always be made that it is better to be right and suffer than to remain silent. On the other hand, it can also be argued that the university's traditional status as a sanctuary—with the corollary provision of academic freedom—is jeopardized whenever the classroom becomes a forum for indoctrination, no matter how worthy the values being taught.

The only certainty is that the young teacher—particularly the humanities teacher—will be in the thick of the fight for the next few years. His decisions will determine the course the humanities take, the conditions under which he works, and finally the place of the humanities in American life. Since the issue here is nothing less than whether we will become a technocracy or remain a civilization, he had better make his decisions with his eyes open.

The Art
of Teaching Science

MORRIS H. SHAMOS

THE TEACHER

With few exceptions the beginning college teacher of science is a graduate student, most often a doctoral candidate. At least this is true of the universities that offer graduate programs in science. In institutions that have no graduate programs, the beginning science teacher may be a part-time graduate student in a nearby university, or more likely he will have had previous teaching experience elsewhere. Very few college teachers of science have only bachelors' degrees and no graduate work (either completed or in progress) in their subject areas.

The characterization of the beginning college teacher of science as a graduate student may come as a surprise to some, particularly to those who have never regarded the teaching assistant in this light. Because of the nature of their duties, many teaching assistants do not feel themselves truly a part of the teaching profession—and in many departments they are not thought of as teachers in the usual sense. Nevertheless, this sort of appointment gives them their first exposure both to some form of teacher-student relationship, however tenuous it may seem, and to a teacher-department relationship. The assistants' attitudes about teaching, in fact their overall impressions of the academic structure, are often crystallized during this experience. Some become strongly motivated by it; others may be just as strongly repelled from teaching careers as a result of unhappy experiences as teaching assistants.

Normally, one thinks of the beginning college teacher as a recent Ph.D. who has received his first professional academic appointment, generally in the rank of instructor or assistant professor. While it is true that such persons are recognized as full-fledged faculty members, whereas graduate teaching assistants are not, one should bear in mind that most of the former were in the ranks of the latter just prior to their full-time academic appointments. There may be a lag of a year or two, for service in postdoctoral research fellowships, but it is

Dr. Shamos is chairman, Department of Physics, New York University, and past-president, National Science Teachers' Association.

quite clear that practically all who enter the college-teaching profession in the field of science had their first tastes of it while serving as teaching assistants—and that such service, in point of time, was but recently removed from their first regular faculty appointments.

Most beginning teachers are young, barely older than the students to whom they probably relate better than they do to most of the senior members of the departments. Their titles vary: teaching assistant, graduate assistant, teaching fellow, or, occasionally, lecturer or instructor. The last two generally imply full-time teaching duties; the others are part-time assignments to allow for graduate study. The past two decades have seen a slight departure from this practice. Because of the availability of federal funds for graduate fellowships and research assistantships in the sciences, some of the most promising students complete their graduate work without having to teach and hence begin teaching somewhat later in their careers, usually at a higher academic level. This change creates a special problem, for it means that such persons must assume in their first teaching positions a greater degree of responsibility and authority than they would first have assumed as regular graduate assistants.

The duties of the latter group vary somewhat according to discipline and institution. In those disciplines in which large laboratory sections are the practice (e.g., biology and chemistry), the experience of a graduate assistant may be limited to assisting a senior member of the department in the laboratory. (Sometimes these sections are large enough to require several graduate assistants.) His work in the laboratory, plus grading laboratory reports and examination papers, may be the only exposure to students that such a graduate assistant will have. This means that he may acquire no significant teaching experience, involving full intellectual contact with students, until his postdoctoral years.

Some departments, notably in physics, have relatively small laboratory sections in their introductory courses and generally have small discussion sections as well. In such departments the graduate assistant has a more challenging assignment since he is often placed in charge of one or more of these sections. This provides mixed blessings. Not all first-year graduate students respond equally well to a challenge in which one is faced with the direct responsibility for a group of students, including evaluation of their performance. While curriculum, text, examinations, and the like are generally the responsibility of a senior faculty member, who also supervises the work of the teaching assistants, the assistants nevertheless have the sort of contact with students, particularly in recitation sections, that is very close to a true teaching experience.

Being on the firing line in this way has the advantage of maturing some teachers very rapidly, although all graduate assistants may not adapt to it readily and may perhaps be somewhat unfair to their students. In general, those graduate assistants who seek academic careers and have a genuine interest in teaching profit most from such an abrupt plunge into a teacher-student relationship. Every department can point to a few of its graduate assistants who show promise of becoming exceptional teachers. For such assistants some measure of independence in the classroom is probably the best training. Others may require a more gradual introduction to teaching. Whatever the case, until one has had the responsibility for guiding a group of students through a major segment of a course, one cannot be said to have truly begun a college-teaching career.

Ultimately, a regular member of the faculty must assume primary responsibility for a given course. Normally, he will be of professorial rank, although in some departments instructors and lecturers may also be given such assignments. If the course is lecture-laboratory, the faculty member in charge generally does the lectures and determines course routine, leaving the laboratory and possibly discussion sections to junior members of the staff, usually to graduate assistants. How much independent judgment he allows them in carrying out their duties depends upon the department and, to some extent, upon the kind of laboratory. In large laboratory sections, for example, graduate assistants may serve as little more than trouble-shooters and graders.

The duties of the graduate assistant, and hence the extent to which he becomes involved in teaching, largely depend upon how his particular department views the position. In the past some science departments regarded it as merely a means of supporting their graduate students; others frankly viewed it as a source of inexpensive help. But many departments looked upon teaching as an essential part of graduate training in science, on the dual grounds that teaching a subject helped one to learn it and that serving as a graduate assistant initiated the prospective academic scientist into what was at one time considered a major function of academic life—namely, teaching. In fact, some departments insisted that every doctoral candidate have some teaching experience during his graduate career.

Customs have changed in the past two decades, partly because of increased numbers of graduate students in the sciences, partly because of increased research funds, and partly because of a greater concern for the welfare of the undergraduate.

The larger number of graduate students makes it impossible for many departments to afford all students an opportunity to teach. This development is not to be regarded as necessarily unfortunate, for it means that preference can be given to those who are primarily interested in academic careers, leaving those who are not interested in teaching to be supported by research funds, fellowships, or other sources. Another reason to prefer future teachers for graduate teaching positions is the increased sensitivity of science departments to the complaints of undergraduates about the teaching skills of graduate assistants. Thus, the graduate teaching-assistantship in most science departments is no longer regarded primarily as a means of supporting graduate students or of securing cheap labor. Instead, there is a growing tendency to look upon it as part of the training of the graduate students who profess an interest in teaching and who also appear to be suited to it. This is not to suggest that the millennium has arrived—that teaching assistants in the sciences are being accorded full faculty privileges and given all the help they need to develop their teaching skills. Far from it! As Wise points out, except for a few institutions the situation is still rather deplorable.[1] Yet the trend is encouraging.

It is not easy to achieve the best balance between teachers and research assistants in a department, as both positions compete for similar talents. The teaching assistantship was once regarded by most graduate students as a prestigious appointment, but the research assistantship has largely supplanted it as a more direct path toward the doctorate. The cutback in research funds during the latter half of 1968 had the effect of suddenly increasing the number of applicants for teaching assistantships. Various departments are experimenting with ways of resolving this dilemma, as well as with the problem of how to make the teaching experience of graduate assistants more meaningful than it has been in the past. It is hoped that new ways will be found to make the work of such assistants in the sciences much more stimulating and rewarding to all concerned with teaching—the graduate assistants, the senior faculty, and the undergraduates.

There are several obvious ways of achieving more effective involvement of teaching assistants in the educational process. One method used by a few science departments is to bring all new teaching assistants to the campus several weeks prior to the opening of classes for a series of briefings, discussions with senior faculty members, and possibly a short course or seminar series devoted to teaching problems and techniques. Another method is to require that all new assistants take, in effect, an in-service teacher-training program during the first semester in residence. Such a program might consist of the same elements mentioned above—that is, briefings, discussions, and methods seminars— perhaps plus the added features of involvement of members of the

1. W. Max Wise, "Who Teaches the Teachers?"

education faculty and observation and evaluation of the teaching assistants on their effectiveness as teachers. Needless to say, if such a program is attempted, the normal duties of the teaching assistants during this period should be reduced accordingly.

Still another approach is to require each teaching assistant, or at least those who profess an interest in academic careers, to take over the course lecture for a day or two toward the end of his first year in the department. Such experience is invaluable to the beginning teacher, for it not only stimulates him but provides both the teacher and senior faculty a means of assessing his potential as a member of the teaching community. There are problems with this approach, of course, particularly the possible resentment of students in the course to having inexperienced lecturers assigned to them. Hence, if used at all, this method requires great care and diplomacy on the part of the senior faculty.

THE STUDENTS

There are three main categories of students who enroll in science courses in our colleges:

1. Pure-science majors, most of whom regard their undergraduate preparation as a form of professional education even though they are found mainly in liberal arts colleges. A large proportion of these students, as many as two-thirds or more in some fields, plan to go on to graduate work. A few go into high-school teaching and the rest go into industry or government laboratories. For the most part the undergraduate curricula for science majors are designed to prepare them for graduate work and professional careers.

2. The applied-science students, who are required to take certain science courses as part of their preprofessional training in a science-related field. These include engineering students, premedical and predental students, other pure-science majors, mathematics majors, and the like. Very often these students are placed in the same courses as the science majors; in some cases special courses or special sections of a course are designated for one or more of these groups. There are cogent arguments for both systems, as is pointed out later.

3. The nonscience students, who generally take science as part of their distribution requirements and who, more often than not, are unhappy about the requirement. This group includes education and commerce students, and in a typical university it comprises more than 90 percent of all students enrolled in the introductory science courses. In some institutions these students are required to take the regular departmental courses designed for science or applied-science majors. In most colleges, however, special courses

are offered for this group, a practice which appears to be growing and which, in recent years, has provoked considerable thought and attention among science faculties and others responsible for formulating educational policy in American colleges.

Those for whom college science is most meaningful are naturally the students who regard it as part of their professional training. These include the pure-science majors and what have been termed applied-science or science-related majors; that is, the engineering, premedical, predental, and similar majors. Usually, much more detailed information and depth of understanding can be expected of these students than one can reasonably expect of nonscience students. This is certainly true of majors, who are after all potential colleagues, and perhaps somewhat less true of the science-related group. The least-common factor that sets both groups apart from the nonscience students is, of course, a professional, if not intellectual, commitment to some branch of science.

THE COURSES

The beginning college teacher usually faces his most challenging assignment in the introductory courses, particularly in those taken by the nonscience students. In fact, teaching an introductory course is probably the most difficult task of any college science-teacher. In most departments the beginning teacher (i.e., graduate assistant) is assigned all his teaching duties in such courses. In the rare instance that a new graduate assistant is given an upper-division assignment, it is invariably as an assistant in a large laboratory-section in which he has little direct responsibility. Hence the following discussion will be limited to the lower-level or first-year courses.

Every science department has an introductory course designed for the "serious" students, departmental majors and, in many instances, other students in science-related fields. Some departments have two such courses, one for departmental majors and the other for the latter group. There are more likely to be two courses in physics or chemistry than in biology or geology. In addition, there may be other introductory courses for special groups of students, e.g., physics for engineers or chemistry for nurses. While course offerings today are probably a good deal less fragmented than they were two or three decades ago, one still finds departments that offer a number of introductory courses, each designed for a particular group of students and differing slightly from the others.

From the point of view of the beginning teacher, there may be important differences among these courses. The difference lies chiefly in the outlook of the students. For example, the interaction between a graduate assistant and a prospective physics major enrolled in an introductory course in the physics department might be quite different from the interaction between the assistant and a premedical student or engineering student enrolled in the same or another first-year physics course. In the former case there is a stronger sense of identity with both the student and the course material. In general, science majors tend to relate well to graduate assistants in their own disciplines, just as they do to their fellow majors. The identification stems from a common professional interest and probably in part from the realization that the time devoted to such courses and students will directly benefit the profession.

Courses that are not designed for majors are usually regarded as *service courses,* a term that somehow carries a pejorative connotation. No science department likes to consider itself primarily involved in providing service courses; there is something impermanent about the idea. Yet most departments are called upon to provide such courses because the number of nonmajors enrolled in a given science department at any one time usually far exceeds the number of majors, as was shown earlier.

As to the difference in content between those courses designed for majors and those designed for special science-related groups of students, it may be no more than a matter of emphasis. For example, an introductory physics course designed for engineering students might differ from the conventional course only in stressing certain examples and subjects of special interest to engineers (e.g., statics, strength of materials) and in using engineering, rather than metric, units. On the other hand, the difference is sometimes fundamental. Frequently, the introductory physics course for majors or engineering students requires calculus as a prerequisite, whereas a course for liberal arts students generally would not require it. This means that there is not only a different emphasis but also a different basic approach. The graduate assistant feels more comfortable when he is involved with the calculus-based course, for it is easier to teach physics when one is free to use appropriate mathematical techniques. This situation is frequent in chemistry, where the laboratory course for majors may require a stronger mathematical background than the corresponding course for nonmajors. It is rarely the case in biology or geology, since the introductory courses are usually open to all students, majors and nonmajors alike. Thus the teacher in these courses must cope with a much wider range of student interest and motivation, a situation that is far from ideal.

In the final group of courses are those designed specifically for nonscience students, the largest bloc of students on any university campus. Here too, as far as the introductory course is concerned, some departments make no distinction between these students and their own majors. The theory is that the best way to help a nonscientist appreciate a given scientific discipline is to expose him to it in the same way as one who is preparing for a career in that discipline. While some nonscience students apparently do benefit from the rigor and professional orientation of a course designed for majors, most do not; and on the whole the theory has been widely discredited.

Most colleges, therefore, offer one or more special courses for their nonscience students. These range from simplified versions of the regular departmental courses to composite courses such as physical science or integrated courses that, in principle, cut across departmental lines. The latter type of survey course has had a checkered history. It is by far the most difficult kind of science course to teach because very few teachers feel equally at home in several science disciplines. As a result, when a single person tries to teach such a course, he tends to stress that area with which he is most familiar, that is, his own discipline.

To overcome this problem, departments sometimes offer such courses as team-teaching efforts, different segments of a course being taught by specialists from the various disciplines. This approach has not proved very successful either, for it depends so much upon how the team members view the purpose of an integrated course and how well they work together. There are also logistic problems for the staff associated with such a course, since only one team member actually teaches at any given time. Scheduling for such courses is easier, for example, in institutions operating on the quarter system than in those on the semester or trimester systems.

Not all courses for nonscience students offer laboratory experience. Some departments apparently believe that the limited experience provided in the short time available cannot be very meaningful and that the time might be better spent in other ways. This is not yet a widespread practice, but the feeling is growing that the routine laboratory exercises characteristic of standard introductory courses are not the best means of demonstrating the experimental approach to such students. Most academic scientists believe that the laboratory is an essential part of science education, but many also believe that the nonscience student deserves special attention in both course design and laboratory experience.

The Goals of Science Education

SCIENTIFIC LITERACY

One of the strangest paradoxes of our times is the great gap between the practice and the teaching of science. This may be a scientific age by some standards, but certainly not if judged by the scientific sophistication of the general population. Incongruous as it may seem for a civilization that is so greatly dependent upon science, Americans are on the whole scientifically illiterate.

Despite the enormous strides the country has made in scientific knowledge, science teaching remains largely an art. Evidently, teachers have not yet discovered either the proper motivating factors or the pedagogical techniques (or both) that are needed for developing true scientific literacy. The scientific community has produced a highly ordered body of knowledge and has developed a methodology that appears to be reasonably successful in guiding it toward a better understanding of nature; yet except for selected groups of students, teachers have not succeeded in imparting this knowledge to others in a meaningful way.

Although both science and nonscience majors are, in a sense, captive students, in the past decade or so concern has been voiced in some quarters that the traditional courses offered them have not kept pace with new developments in the sciences. In an effort to improve college science courses and curriculums, eight college science commissions have been established in recent years.[2] These are independent, ad hoc organizations, which have two primary goals: to update the content of undergraduate courses and to bring to bear on them the same sort of inquiring attitude that is characteristic of creative research. Activities vary among the commissions, but in general their concerns range from preprofessional education to general education for nonscience students. An instructor or department considering a course or curriculum revision would be well advised to examine the reports of the appropriate commission before making any changes.

While the commissions do maintain an interest in the nonscience student, he is not their primary concern, and his problem has not been tackled in a fully organized fashion. Yet it is, in a way, the most pressing problem in science education today. We will return to the question of curriculum development for nonscience students.

Practically every college requires its students to take some science

2. Advisory Council on College Chemistry, Department of Chemistry, Stanford University, Stanford, Calif. 94305; Commission on College Geography, Eastern Michigan University, Ypsilanti, Mich. 48197; Commission on College Physics, Department of Physics and Astronomy, University of Maryland, 4321 Hartwick Rd., College Park, Md. 20740; Commission on Education in Agriculture and Natural Resources, 2102 Constitution Ave. NW, Washington, D.C. 20418; Council on Education in the Geological Sciences, 1444 N St. NW, Washington, D.C. 20005; Commission on Engineering Education, 1501 New Hampshire Ave. NW, Washington, D.C. 20036; Commission on Undergraduate Education in the Biological Sciences, 1717 Massachusetts Ave. NW, Washington, D.C. 20036; Committee on the Undergraduate Program in Mathematics, P.O. Box 1024, Berkeley, Calif. 94701.

as part of a liberal education, whether or not they are interested in this phase of man's intellectual activity. In the past it was taken for granted that science was one of the "cultural imperatives" of a college education. Today one hears serious challenges to this practice on the ground that if the science that is presented to nonscience students makes so little impact on them, why should it be required. This criticism has forced the academic community to reexamine the goals of education for the nonscience student.

BACKGROUND FOR MODERN LIFE

Why do schools teach science to all students? Clearly, they do not teach it only to produce scientists and engineers, for there are too few of them to justify the massive effort in contemporary science education. Schools insist that all students be exposed to science, yet more than 90 percent of all students are not science bound and will not in their adult lives have any direct contact with science in a formal way. Hence one cannot reasonably argue that compulsory science education satisfies a practical need of society, just as one cannot justify most of what is taught in the liberal arts on utilitarian grounds.

Thus the purpose of science education for nonscience students must be primarily intellectual rather than utilitarian. Schools teach science, as they teach most disciplines, to acquaint students with the world in which they live—with the aesthetic as well as the real world. How the students ultimately cope intellectually with the real world depends largely upon how comfortably they fit into it, that is, upon how well they appreciate man's efforts to understand and control nature.

It follows that the main goal of science education for nonscience students should be to provide them with the sort of background they will need to function as informed, literate adults in modern society. This is much easier said than done, as must be evident from many decades of fruitless effort. If one confines himself to specific objectives, the task is a good deal simpler, except that those objectives which one can easily test are almost certain to fall in the *cognitive* domain and are very likely to be trivial. The reason is obvious: it is much easier to test for factual knowledge than for intellectual skills such as analysis and synthesis. And the latter, in turn, are easier to evaluate than are the long-range objectives that relate to scientific literacy. Such objectives fall mainly in the *affective* domain, as seen in the following example.

In 1966 the Educational Policies Commission of the National Education Association issued a report that sought to define the "spirit of science" and to urge schools to promote understanding of the values on which all science is based. The report, which was the product of a group of distinguished scientists and educators, lists the following values underlying science:

1. Longing to know and to understand.
2. Questioning of all things.
3. Search for data and their meaning.
4. Demand for verification.
5. Respect for logic.
6. Consideration of premises.
7. Consideration of consequences. [3]

Note that the values do not refer specifically to science but clearly would be desirable outcomes of any educational program. One could wish for little more than to have such values generally guide the thoughts and actions of educated men. The fact that these attitudes are particularly evident in the practice of science is sometimes given as an argument in favor of some science education for all.

The general nature of these statements should also be noted. They reflect attitudes or values, as do all substantive goals of liberal education. To these might be added such obvious objectives as appreciation for the nature of science, understanding of the role of science in man's intellectual development, and so on. All are *affective* goals, for which teachers have no simple means of testing; nor do teachers know how to design curriculums that may lead to such objectives. This point cannot be emphasized too strongly. Specifying educational goals is relatively easy, whether they be cognitive or affective goals. Designing a curriculum that promises to achieve these goals is much more difficult—and more difficult still is the designing of effective test instruments to measure the achievement of these goals, particularly in the affective domain.

The problem is further complicated by the fact that the primary goal one seeks when confronted with the question of scientific literacy is a long-range rather than an immediate objective. Hence testing the effectiveness of a given curriculum in its contribution to general scientific literacy in adults is clearly very difficult, if even possible in an objective fashion. In view of these difficulties, perhaps all that can be done when designing a curriculum for nonscience students is simply to keep in mind the lessons of the past. It is well known, for example, that nonscience students tend to avoid quantitative science-courses in favor of the more qualitative or descriptive courses. Thus, where a free choice is permitted, they favor biology and geology over physics and chemistry, with physics invariably the last choice.

3. The Educational Policies Commission, *Education and the Spirit of Science.*

UNDERSTANDING THE ROLE OF MATHEMATICS

The tendency of students to shy away from mathematics, even when it is used merely as a tool, must be counted as a major reason why students seek to avoid certain science courses. Most students do not fully appreciate either the power of mathematics as a system of logic or the nature of its role as the language of science. In face, it is a serious failing of almost all academic science that mathematics is portrayed primarily as a tool for solving problems in science. This is the popular notion, one that is harmful both to the cause of science and to mathematics.

The physicist P. W. Bridgman once pointed out "that the fundamental human invention is language, and that we owe the progress of the race to it more than to anything else." [4] In a similar sense, mathematics is also a language, and the progress of science is more indebted to it than to anything else.

Mathematics is the language of science, the only language available by which statements about nature can be combined according to formal, logical rules; a language which not only allows one to describe in precise terms the world about him but also provides a means of dealing with the descriptions that may lead to new knowledge of the universe. It is an essential part of the structure of science, not simply an accessory or tool. Physics, for example, could not have developed to its present stage without mathematics—and the life sciences will not achieve the same level of sophistication until they have established a firm mathematical foundation. This should be borne in mind whenever one reflects on the goals of science education, for surely one of the goals ought to be a clear understanding of the role of mathematics in the scientific enterprise.

DEVELOPMENT OF MEANINGFUL CURRICULA

The major problem in contemporary science-education is the provision of meaningful courses for nonscience students. There has been no major effort that could compare with the massive curriculum-development projects in science for the elementary and secondary schools during the past decade, practically all of which were funded by federal agencies. Instead, with one or two exceptions such as the PSNS Project,[5] curriculum development in college-level science has been on a much more limited and individualized scale. Descriptions of some of the programs may be found in the newsletters published by the several college

4. P. W. Bridgman, *The Nature of Physical Theory*, p. 17.
5. Physical Science for Nonscience Students, L. G. Bassett, director, Rensselaer Polytechnic Institute, Troy, N.Y.

commissions. The PSNS Project, for example, grew out of a number of conferences sponsored by the Commission on College Physics, with the cooperation of the Advisory Council on College Chemistry. Others are described from time to time in the various journals devoted primarily to science teaching, e.g., *American Journal of Physics, Journal of Chemical Education*. But perhaps the best guides to current trends in course development are the texts and supplementary readings that have been published in recent years.

For the most part, the texts and supplementary materials that depart from the usual format tend to concentrate on a few major topics, to go into these in greater depth, and to stress the development and structure of the discipline rather than minute details. The choice of topics may differ, reflecting as it does the designers' views of the course, but the common element is readily discernible: an emphasis on ideas rather than on pure factual knowledge. This is particularly evident in the supplementary-reading materials presently available, especially the paperbacks, many of which deal with only a single topic.

The fact that the great ideas or conceptual schemes of science are total abstractions and that many of them require stretching one's imagination beyond the limits of common sense appears not to trouble the nonscience student as much as does solving problems or committing to memory such factual material as systems of units, conversion factors, classification systems, and so forth. By playing down the routine problem-solving and pure memorization, which after all are really unimportant to anyone but professional scientists or those preparing for careers in science, the course makes more time available for dealing with substantive ideas. The nonscience students apparently find such courses much more palatable than the older courses. This is not to say that mathematical demonstration must be completely abandoned. On the contrary, some of the new courses maintain reasonable mathematical rigor but simply minimize the problem-solving skills normally required of students in the physical sciences.

Thus, the general trend appears to be away from the survey course and toward in-depth focus on one topic, or perhaps a few topics at most. There is also a discernible tendency to include more history of science in such courses, somewhat reminiscent of Conant's famous case history techniques.[6] This is not suggested as a substitute for science proper, but rather as a supplement to it—one that somehow appeals to students generally and that might be considered by the new teacher as an effective means of gaining student interest. Where term papers or reports are assigned in such courses, it is often useful to suggest that students write these on the history of the subject, rather than on some

6. James Bryant Conant, ed., *Harvard Case Histories in Experimental Science.*

contemporary phase. Since the history of science is largely descriptive, students usually feel more comfortable with it and find doing such a paper more an enjoyment than a chore.

Techniques of Teaching Science

There is a characteristic difference between the basic technique of teaching science and that used in teaching almost any other academic discipline, namely, the extensive use of demonstration. Whether demonstration is used in the classic sense of lecture demonstrations or with chalkboards and other visual aids, it is striking how much more science teaching depends upon the visual sense than upon the auditory. Even the tutorial or discussion sessions commonly used in certain disciplines (e.g., physics) are demonstrative in the sense that they develop skills in problem solving or reinforce the students' understanding of the subject matter. It is virtually impossible when teaching science to communicate with students by the spoken word alone. One always needs some means of visual exposition. This sometimes presents a problem in institutions that have common classroom facilities; a room suitable for a course in literature or history may be wholly unsuited for a science course because of inadequate board space. Room-assignment clerks do not always appreciate this difference and usually must be educated to it by the uncompromising demands of the science faculty.

Good facilities for science teaching are, by comparison with other disciplines, far more costly in both space and money—a fact that does not go unnoticed by nonscience departments in the competition for university funds. The additional space is required mainly for the laboratories, with their attendant stockrooms and service shops (e.g., machine shops, electronic shops, glass-working shops). The higher cost is accounted for largely by equipment, supplies, and the technicians needed to staff the various shops and stockrooms.

For the science major there appears to be no satisfactory substitute for direct laboratory experience. There are differences of opinion on the relative merits of "even-front" laboratories with all students doing the same experiment during a given lab period and of individualized laboratories with each student or student pair working on a different experiment and rotating each week from one to another. The individualized laboratory has the advantages of providing a greater diversity of experiments for a given equipment budget and an opportunity to conduct open-ended laboratories. There are disadvantages for the instructor, of course, and in some science disciplines such a system may be quite impractical. However, there does appear to be a trend toward the individualized laboratory, particularly in physics, where laboratory equipment tends to be fairly costly and where they have long been the practice in advanced courses.

As for laboratories for nonscience students, the question remains open. Some teachers do not believe that the laboratory is an effective instructional technique for this group. Others, and these probably constitute the majority, believe that the laboratory is essential to teaching any science, but many would concede that new patterns must be found to make the laboratory a more meaningful instructional tool for nonscience students.

THE NEW TECHNOLOGY

Of all the new audiovisual aids that have been developed in the past decade or so, closed-circuit television holds the most promise for science education. Closed-circuit television is solving one of the major problems of the large science lecture-hall by bringing lecture demonstrations, regardless of size, close to every student in the class. This is accomplished by placing monitors throughout the lecture hall, usually suspended from the ceiling, and using one or two cameras at the lecture table. The one drawback at the moment is the lack of color, which may be very important for certain types of demonstrations, but color is probably not too far in the future. Closed-circuit television may soon invade the laboratory as well. One can imagine, for example, that all the microscopes in a biology laboratory will be equipped with individual cameras and monitors, as many research microscopes are today.

Many of the functions of slide and overhead projectors can be taken over by closed-circuit television once a lecture hall has been equipped with monitors. One advantage of this system over the overhead projector, assuming that color is not a critical factor, is that it can also be used to project opaque objects or materials. Thus, when properly installed, closed-circuit television can replace all forms of still projection as well as provide close-ups of lecture demonstrations, and it can do so with convenience for the instructor. It takes little imagination to see this as the single visual-aid system of the future, although its use today is still small compared with the more conventional visual-aid devices.

The use of computer-assisted instruction and other self-training devices (e.g., programmed texts) has not yet had much impact on science teaching at the college level. Some courses have been programmed, and a few programmed texts have appeared, but on the whole the academic community seems unwilling to experiment very broadly with the new educational technology. There is little doubt that in the development of skills (e.g., mathematical skills, problem solving in physics or chemistry, classifications, morphology) educational technology can play a significant role. Hence, the computer will no doubt become a routine adjunct to the classroom of the future. However, as was pointed out earlier, the truly important goals of science education are not simply skills, nor do they fall in the cognitive domain. This means that until science educators discover how to specify affective goals in behavioral terms, so that the resources of educational technology may be brought to bear on the problem, one cannot look to computer-assisted instruction as a panacea for science education, or even as providing a fresh path to scientific literacy.

EXAMINATIONS AND GRADES

It is sometimes said that for most students a college education consists mainly of sporadic preparation for examinations. There is a large measure of truth in the statement, for our educational system demands that teachers evaluate students in some way, and the so-called objective examination has become the major evaluative instrument on which course grades are based.

The trouble with objective examinations—and the sciences are perhaps more at fault here than most other disciplines—is that they test little more than a student's power of recall. The more objective an examination is, the more factual it is bound to be and the less its value as a means of measuring understanding or appreciation of important ideas in science.

One can easily evaluate a skill such as laboratory technique by direct observation—or skill in problem solving by objective examination. And it may be that for the science major the discipline fostered by such examinations is a valuable part of his professional training. Even this supposition is debatable, for not all students respond equally well to the pressure of written examinations, and some of those who do not do well may be highly qualified for careers in science. Students deserve every possible opportunity to demonstrate their abilities by whatever means are necessary: open-book examinations where factual recall is unimportant, personal interviews or oral examinations, laboratory reports, term papers, and so on. Since teachers are compelled to assign grades, a useful technique is to permit each student to select from among several evaluative instruments a given number on which his grade will be based. While perhaps not ideal, this is a fairer way of judging students than most systems that are used.

One might even challenge the entire concept of grades and grading systems, as many have done recently, for the evidence is that at best the correlation between college grades and success in life is very tenuous.[7] However, until a better way is found to provide students with some measure of their progress and to compare them with one another, teachers must make the best of the present system. At the very least, one should recognize the injustice of reading numerical grades too literally (e.g., distinguishing between 80 and 85) or of using any grading system with gradations too fine to be meaningful.

The pass-fail option, which has now been adopted by a number of colleges, has proved to be a particular boon to the sciences insofar as the nonscience student is concerned. Students who have a particular fear of science or who believe they will not do well in the courses can, by electing this option, take their science in a relaxed frame of mind and without being overly concerned about their overall grade-average, since pass-fail courses are normally not included in the averaging process.

There are cogent arguments against the pass-fail system that deserve careful consideration. One is that it encourages academic laziness in students. Another is that a student's final record will not be a true indicator of his performance or ability if he elects the pass-fail option at every opportunity. To counter such arguments one might point out that at the college level it is more important that a student do very well in his major field (in which the pass-fail option usually is not permitted) than do only moderately well in all subject areas. Moreover, the modern concept of a liberal education leans more heavily on a meaningful exposure to several diverse branches of knowledge than on mastery of each. It seems to me that, on balance, the advantages of the pass-fail system, especially in science, far outweigh any problems it may create. One may hope that this practice will soon spread to all colleges and perhaps ultimately to the high schools.

The new teacher normally has little to say about the grading practices in his department or college. However, the entire question of evaluating student performance is so central to the education process that one can hardly think of developing new science curriculums (for nonscience students, for example) without considering the forms of evaluation that might be used to assess the programs. The new teacher, being so close to his own student days, can contribute a great deal to the dialog on this subject. He should make every effort to at least keep the issue alive in his department and to persuade his colleagues that the problem warrants much consideration.

SHOWMANSHIP

Teaching is an art. There is little that is scientific about it—even in the sciences. The new teacher in the sciences has contact mainly with

7. Dael Wolfle, *Science* editorial.

beginning students, who may be science majors or not. These students are highly impressionable. They have not become jaded in the academic sense, particularly not in science. The image that the teacher creates in the minds of these students can be a major factor in his success with them.

In the theater one must be a showman to win his audience. There is something almost magic about the rapport that exists between the great performer and his audience. There is an element of showmanship in successful teaching as well. This does not mean that one must be a performer, although there are notable examples of highly successful lecturers in the sciences who plan their lecture-demonstrations as much for dramatic impact as instructional value. In fact, lecture-demonstrations in science, conducted as they usually are in large, impersonal lecture halls, need something of this sort to maintain student interest at a high level, particularly for nonscience students. Every science teacher should give some thought to the thespian quality of his work.

But the beginning teacher rarely has the opportunity to practice showmanship. His contact with students is more personal; hence, his showmanship must be of a different sort. He establishes a rapport with students primarily through his sensitivity to their problems. It is no longer fashionable for college teachers to remain aloof from their students, and the beginning teacher must be particularly careful not to seem condescending to his students. Regardless of how he may feel about the intellectual or personality deficiencies of a group of students, the mark of a good teacher is his ability to conceal these feelings and play the role of an understanding guide who is genuinely interested in the academic welfare of his students.

Establishing this kind of rapport with students is showmanship in the social and intellectual sense rather than in the sense of dramatic performance. The relationship is charismatic rather than awe-inspiring. The beginning teacher can serve as a model of intellectual and personal development, as one who is not far removed in age or outlook from most of his students. He can, if he is so inclined, guide students to emulate his own emerging career. However trite it may seem, those who serve as teaching assistants in the sciences have reached a certain level of recognition for their intellectual achievements and may be able to inspire students to similar attainments.

The wise teacher will show that he understands both the power of formal instruction and the dynamics of contemporary student-life. He will make a studied effort, to go beyond the classroom in his interaction with students—to make himself a part of both their intellectual and campus lives. To be successful at it, he somehow must display the full range of his intellectual skill and curiosity, not only his knowledge of science. And this is probably best done in an informal social setting rather than in the classroom. It is time-consuming and may seem unproductive to the beginning teacher; but it is very important to students.

Some teachers have a flair for such a role. They can be firm yet gentle in their handling of students. They regard every question from a student as meriting a sincere, reasoned reply, regardless of how absurd or unintelligent the question may be. Ridicule is a self-defeating pedagogical device, one that has no place in the classroom. The new teacher should be very conscious of the respect and admiration that he commands; these will depend not only upon his mastering the subject matter but also on his mastering the art of teaching. It is an art worth cultivating by anyone who seeks an academic career.

Is Science Relevant?

On college campuses these are days of reassessment. Students have become more vocal, more demanding with regard to their role in the academic community. It matters little that the more strident voices belong to a small minority; the whole academic world has been caught up in the pressure for change, and the prevailing mood appears to be a willingness of faculties and administrations to experiment with new approaches to all sorts of academic problems.

What does this mean for the new science teacher? It means, first of all, a subtle change in the traditional teacher-student relationship, one that strangely enough often tends to bring the two closer together than they were in the past. The change is probably less obvious to the new teacher, who is himself freshly removed from the student category, than to the old. Virtually all faculties have become sensitive to the mood for change. They (reluctantly) accept student course and faculty evaluations as part of normal campus life—once the initial shock of the new student-militancy has worn off. They more or less accept student representation on faculty committees and student participation in university governance.

Among the student demands, one often hears a call for more *relevant* education—more relevant to the times, to social and political problems, and to the students' lives. Whatever one may think of the merits of these demands, it is proper to ask how the study of science may be considered relevant to the lives of students. I do not believe that relevancy should be the main, or even a necessary, criterion for liberal education. Nevertheless, since some students are raising this question, it is important that colleges try to answer it.

Obviously, the question has little meaning to science majors or even to students in science-related programs. Both of these groups see science as being directly related to their professional careers. Those for whom the question is most meaningful are the nonscience students, many of whom believe that science is too remote from everyday life to warrant its inclusion among the "cultural imperatives." This group, as well as the majority of the adult population, sees science largely through its end products, through the technology that turns on its discoveries. We are literally surrounded by the material products of science. Our habits, our modes of life, our health, our ability to wage war or encourage peace—all are conditioned by advances in technology. These advances, moreover, result generally from specific needs of society. Against such a background it is not surprising that control of nature (i.e., technology) is so often confused with man's desire to understand it, which is the main goal of science.

What is most relevant to nonscience students is technology. They are interested in the things they read about in the newspapers or see on television—advances in medicine (or anything affecting their health), missiles, space travel, fluoridation, air and water pollution, or bomb testing, for example. They want to discuss the social and philosophical aspects of science, possibly because they can express opinions on these matters whereas they cannot on science.

The danger in designing courses primarily responsive to the demand for relevancy is that the content may be so peripheral to the intellectual goals of science as to mislead students on the true nature of this branch of learning. Moreover, few teachers of science can also represent themselves as being expert in such areas as philosophy or the social sciences. Unfortunately, the authority that a teacher represents in his special field is often extended by students to encompass all matters discussed in the classroom. Thus there is a very real danger of transference of authority when discussing, for example, social problems having a scientific base.

One of the areas that nonscience students seem to find particularly fascinating might better be termed pseudoscience. They are interested in science fiction, in the occult, in parapsychic phenomena, flying saucers, alchemy, astrology, in all the beliefs and practices which through the ages have existed on the fringe of science and have been nurtured by man's ignorance and gullibility. One cannot easily dispose of these subjects by a wave of the hand. I would venture to say that in the present campus climate most students, given a choice between a course in science and one in science fiction, for example, would probably choose the latter.

This attitude is somewhat understandable, for to the average nonscience student most of science probably seems strange and mysterious. Such students are not persuaded as much by the power of logical

thought as by subject matters that permit free reign of the imagina
To some students this is what is meant by relevancy, that is, anythin
that is fanciful and way out. For others such topics hold some intrinsic
interest, as they do for most people, but while they may be suitable
topics for term papers these students would not insist that they should
form the nucleus of a science course. At the same time, practically all
students believe that the interaction of science and society should be
a part of any science course designed for nonscience students.

This is not to suggest that such topics have no place in the science
curriculum. On the contrary, since they apparently do interest students,
particularly nonscience students, there should be a place for them in the
curriculum. One simply should not permit such discussions to cloud
the main purpose of science education—to portray the nature of the
scientific enterprise. Furthermore, it should be made clear to students
that in these areas the instructor is not necessarily any more expert
than the ordinary educated adult. Students should realize that a
scientist can also have a social conscience, and they might be advised
to examine the extensive literature available on the subject particularly the *Bulletin of the Atomic Scientists*.

One way of resolving this problem is to devote a definite portion
of each class period, say, ten minutes, to a free-wheeling discussion of
any topic related in some way to science. In this way students can
talk out their concerns and opinions on a variety of subjects without
unduly sacrificing the time available for the course content. Another
solution, of course, is to permit the use of such peripheral topics for term
papers and reports in which the student is evaluated, not on how well
he conforms to established scientific thought, but on how well he
defends whatever position he chooses to espouse.

Works Cited

Bridgman, P. W. *The Nature of Physical Theory*. Princeton: Princeton University Press, 1936.

Conant, James Bryant, ed. *Harvard Case Histories in Experimental Science*.
Cambridge: Harvard University Press, 1957.

Educational Policies Commission, The. *Education and the Spirit of Science*.
Washington: National Education Association, 1966.

Wise, W. Max. "Who Teaches the Teachers?" In *Improving College Teaching*,
edited by Calvin B. T. Lee. Washington: American Council on Education,
1967.

Wolfle, Dael. Editorial in *Science* 161 (1968).

A Path
to Relevant Teaching

GARRETT HARDIN

If I see correctly, we are at the beginning of a monumental struggle for the control of the biology curriculum, and more particularly for the control of general education courses in biology. Two visions contend for the orientation of these courses: *molecular biology* and *ecology*. Molecular biology aims at analysis on the finest scale; its goal is to explain the functions of an organism in terms of the architecture of its molecules. Ecology, by contrast, employs a global approach; it attempts to explain the interactions of organisms with each other and with the environment, to uncover the significance of each species in the life of others.

Within ecology there is a rapidly developing subdivision called human ecology. Those who identify themselves as human ecologists have a temperamental liking for Protagoras's aphorism "Man is the measure of all things." This statement should not be thought of as a theory, a hypothesis, or even a convention; it merely expresses the attitude of human ecologists who seek to discover the human significance of the living world.

MOLECULAR BIOLOGY'S POSITION

At the moment molecular biology is on top. In the late 1950s hundreds of college and high school biology teachers joined together under the aegis of the Biological Sciences Curriculum Study (BSCS) to modernize the high school biology courses. During the several years that it took to write the three texts and the many auxiliary books and pamphlets that came out of BSCS in Boulder, Colorado, the molecular code of heredity was deciphered by researchers elsewhere. Under these circumstances it is completely understandable that the topic of molecular biology should have come to occupy the place of honor in the BSCS texts. During the 1960s universities across the country reorganized their biology departments in such a way as to emphasize molecular biology. This also is understandable.

If we regard all the studies that took place before 1953 as part of the embryology of the subject, we can say that Watson and Crick's

Dr. Hardin is professor of biology, University of California, Santa Barbara.

paper on DNA marked the birth of molecular biology. That means the field is now less than twenty years old. A historian of science might suppose that the study is still in the first flush of its youth. This may not be the case. So great is the acceleration of intellectual progress in our time that already molecular biology shows signs of aging, if not senility.

Evidence for this shocking statement is found in the title (and contents) of an evaluative article by one of its leading research practitioners, Gunther S. Stent, "That Was the Molecular Biology That Was." Stent, a student of the physicist-turned-biologist, Max Delbrück of the California Institute of Technology, entered the field early and was "in on the kill." He found it tremendously exciting, and yet by 1967 he was speaking of molecular biology in the past tense. As far as he was concerned, the party was over. It was time to move to other fields, where the grass was greener. Stent's memoirs excited a great deal of interest, and much comment—but no one seriously challenged his basic conclusion that the golden age of molecular biology was over.

Those who plan the future educational offerings of university departments should remember the experience of the Ford Motor Company. In the 1950s Ford brought out a new car in the middle price range, the Edsel. It was a tremendous flop. The company lost some $50 million. There were several reasons for this debacle, but the most important seems to have been that this car was brought out at the wrong time. By the time the first model finally came off the assembly line, independent marketing studies had shown that the demand for medium price cars was going down. The Edsel was out of phase with historical trends.

It begins to look as though the great emphasis on molecular biology in biology curricula is also out of phase with historical realities. Departments, caught in the mesh of committee decisions, typically take five years to revamp their courses. By the time molecular biology was introduced into the curricula, the cry of relevance was in the air. Molecular biology is marvelously exciting and very important at the most fundamental level—but is it relevant? That is, it is relevant to the most pressing concerns of the average student—who is no longer a passive recipient of knowledge?

Many have doubted its relevance. Some have pointed out that, when the traditional courses which emphasized anatomy and taxonomy were displaced by molecular biology, the reform often meant merely that the necessity of memorizing anatomical terms and species names was replaced by the necessity of memorizing the Krebs cycle and the genetic codons. The gain in relevance is not obvious to people standing outside the field of research, that is, to 90 percent of the people who take biology courses.

Some of the promised fruits of molecular biology—for example, the cure for cancer and the molecular control of heredity—are, it is true, quite exciting to John Q. Citizen. If the promises are made good, he will be delighted to accept the results. But in the meantime he has little interest in the technical details. Teachers who are most sensitive to the interests of the nonprofessional student are increasingly looking to the other end of the biological spectrum for guidance in the teaching of their general biology courses; that is, to the ecological end.

ECOLOGY'S FUTURE

The problems and the general orientation of ecology make immediate sense to the average citizen. Warren Weaver has defined biology as "the science of organized complexity." It is apparent to everyone that the most important problems facing us in the future are tied up with the organization of this complexity of species and processes. Population, competition, aggression, pollution, informational systems, and the control of crowd diseases and informational overload—all these are easily recognized as the recalcitrant problems of our time. They are all part of the realm of ecology.

The teacher of college courses in general biology faces a number of serious tactical problems. He must first accept the awkward fact that his personal field of research may not be what the student wants most to hear about. In the past such a basic fact was largely ignored by many teachers who unthinkingly expected their students to be enthusiastic over the teachers' research. Whether students in the future will or will not so adjust themselves to the teachers' desires, it is all too obvious that they do not do so now. The risk of a successful student revolt is all too imminent. For this practical reason, if for no other, it behooves the teacher to ask himself, What is relevant? That is, what is relevant to the interest of the student who is keenly concerned with the world's problems?

Ecology is relevant. It is exciting and rewarding to teach. It is also somewhat frightening. Paul B. Sears has called ecology "the subversive science," a label taken by Paul Shepard and Daniel McKinley for the title of a collection of reprints in ecology. Anyone who sets out to discuss the human implications of ecology soon discovers that the imputation is correct.

Consider, for example, the matter of population. Perhaps the most important single conclusion of population theory is that the growth of human populations must soon be brought to zero (if not below zero for a while) and must never again rise significantly above zero. This simple and unavoidable conclusion strikes at the very basis of the particular type of economic society in which we live. Every arrangement, every maneuver in our economic system presupposes the normality of perpetual growth. Whether the system can survive the necessary adjustment to a zero-growth rate is an open question, one which the biologist cheerfully leaves the economists to wrestle with. That we need to adopt a zero-growth rate is only one among many of the subversive conclusions of the human ecologist. Anyone who teaches a general biology course along ecological lines must expect to find himself fairly continuously on the firing line. He must learn how to survive under attack.

Such, we might say, is the external problem of the biology teacher. His internal problems are no less serious, though somewhat more subtle. Why does one teach anyway? Why should one teach? What does one hope to get out of teaching? There is no reason to think that these questions have definitive answers, but a number of partial answers can be perceived.

WHY TEACH?

One of the primary reasons that anyone teaches is in order to learn. That one does learn by teaching is the universal testimony of all teachers. It is quite possible that one of the dimly felt motivations of every teacher is a desire to learn a subject more thoroughly, which he can do by trying to teach it to someone else. As Jerold Zacharias has said, "If I cannot explain it to you, then I do not understand it myself"—so, let me try to explain it to you.

In the process of trying to explain the semiknown, a teacher may discover that that which is unclear to him is, in fact, unclear to everybody. As that nineteenth-century Renaissance man Alexander von Humboldt said, "It is not possible to lecture on science as science without at the same time comprehending it anew, and it would be incredible if sometimes, perhaps often, one did not come across new discoveries." The necessity of making esoteric knowledge into exoteric knowledge (whether by means of lectures or by popular writing) has led many people to new contributions to knowledge. J. B. S. Haldane, for one, has testified that his daily newspaper columns were the source of some of his most important ideas. Publishable discoveries are an important fringe benefit of taking teaching seriously.

Some teachers, perhaps only a minority, are interested in the processes of teaching and learning themselves. For those with teaching as a major interest, the classroom is a laboratory and the students are the instruments. It is a most striking fact that the most imperfect instruments are the most valuable. John Holt, a superb teacher of small children, has said that "everything I learn about teaching I learn from the bad students." [1]

1. *How Children Fail*, p. 58.

I can bear witness to this truth. The most rewarding class I ever taught was one which I assembled by letting my colleagues know that I was offering a special section to which I would admit only students who hated science. I got them. It was the most stimulating class I ever had. Their aggressive honesty made me see more deeply into my science than I ever had before.

Some teach because they are interested in students. I am sure that the great mass of the taxpayers assume that this is the primary interest of the real teachers, and the best interest. Possibly it is, but there are reasons for seriously questioning whether an all-compelling interest in students is desirable. The psychiatrist Leslie H. Farber has broached the issue in the following terms: "Despite the modern tendency to regard all teaching relationships as primarily interpersonal in character, it is obvious that a teacher's primary dedication must be not to his students but to his subject matter. Were this not so teaching would consist only of those romantic relations, based on vanity or power, which the psychotherapist has learned to call 'transference' situations." [2]

Once we put the act of teaching into a psychiatric framework, insights gained in the analyst-patient relationship cast light upon the teacher-student relationship. Sigmund Freud, for example, has said, "The idea that a neurotic is suffering from a sort of ignorance, and that if one removes the ignorance by telling him facts . . . he must recover, is an idea that has long been superseded, and one derived from superficial appearances. The pathological factor is not his ignorance in itself, but the root of this ignorance in his *inner resistances;* it was they that first called this ignorance into being, and they still maintain it now." [3]

There can be little doubt that inner resistances are at the bottom of most nonlearning—far more often than is mere stupidity. Lawrence S. Kubie has pointed to the relevance of the phenomenon of the *idiot-savant.* How does it come about that a person of extremely limited mentality can show the most fantastic ability to memorize or learn certain sorts of material? Kubie has said that this is because an idiot-savant, like a person under hypnosis, is "so nearly free of conflict as to be able to record preconsciously . . . and thus is able to produce extraordinary feats of memory, of lightning calculations, etc. Occasionally one encounters a man or child whose preconscious learning processes, through some happy accident, operate freely. He learns

2. *Psychiatry* 21 (1958): 19.
3. Cited by Karl Menninger, *Theory of Psychoanalytic Technique* (New York: Basic Books, 1958), p. 103.

effortlessly. To the consternation and anger of his classmates he wins highest grades in a heavy schedule without studying." [4]

It is really very disturbing when you stop to think of it (if you are genuinely interested in students themselves) to realize that the vast majority of our students—certainly well over 99 percent of them—never achieve more than a small fraction of their potential, where potential is thought of as some sort of naked I.Q. The study of people under hypnosis and of idiot-savants gives us some idea of what education might be if we were dealing with students free of disabling conflicts. Perceiving the vast gap between potentiality and reality, we cannot but agree with the philosopher Alfred North Whitehead that "when one considers in its length and in its breadth the importance of this question of the education of a nation's young, the broken lives, the defeated hopes, the national failures, which result from the frivolous inertia with which it is treated, it is difficult to restrain within onself a savage rage." [5]

Yet what are we do to? Whatever we do, it is undoubtedly essential that we keep the deepest problems to ourselves, that we not burden the student with them. Many true things are better not said. Vis-à-vis the student we had better act as if the whole truth were as stated by Farber, that "a teacher's primary dedication must be not to his students but to his subject matter." [6] The reason for adopting this working procedure is deep-grounded in biology. Anyone who has worked with the higher apes has learned the inadvisability of insistently facing an ape directly, of demanding eye-to-eye contact. Resentment, fear, and aggression are the ape's responses to the experimenter's insistence.

Noli me tangere ("touch me not") is the classic Latin verbalization of this universal resentment of an intrusion into the private self. The biological basis of the feeling is deeper than words. To work productively with a learning animal you must focus his attention (and yours) outside the privacy of his deep and important needs, fastening it upon the objects of the world. The human animal is not significantly different from any other in this regard. In the beginning, and most of the time thereafter, our greatest successes in teaching are achieved by indirection, by avoiding too personal a contact. Most of what we know of the students' needs we must keep to ourselves.

The teacher who tries to achieve too personal a contact will be spotted by the sensitive student as one who should be suspected of desires based on vanity or power. To seek transference, even unconsciously, is to arouse defenses on the part of the student.

One more thing must be said, though it must never be said to the

4. *Neurotic Distortion of the Creative Process,* p. 124.
5. *The Aims of Education,* p. 26.
6. *Psychiatry* 21 (1958) : 19.

student. The ideal relationship, the relationship in which the student enjoys the greatest freedom from conflict, is a relationship which follows as a consequence of an act of affiliation by the student. *Affiliation* comes from the Latin word *filius,* "son." To achieve his maximum potential the student must, for a time, become as a son to one whose competence justifies the voluntary abandonment of egoistic resistances. It must be a voluntary affiliation, one not imposed by authority or even achieved by pedagogic seduction. The affiliation must be a consequence of the student's seeing the teacher at his very best. Whitehead has stated the issue most succinctly. "It should be the chief aim of a university professor to exhibit himself in his own true character—that is, as an ignorant man thinking." [7] The student who affiliates himself to such a man has no fear of discovering feet of clay—nor of uncovering evidence of intellectual seduction, for there is none. To such a one the student *grants* authority—and thus becomes free to learn.

7. *The Aims of Education,* p. 48.

Bibliography

Erikson, Erik H. *Identity: Youth and Crisis.* New York: W. W. Norton & Co., 1968.

Holt, John. *How Children Fail.* New York: Pitman Publishing Corp., 1964.

Kubie, Lawrence. *Neurotic Distortion of the Creative Process.* Lawrence, Kans.: University of Kansas Press, 1958.

Platt, John. *The Excitement of Science.* Boston: Houghton Mifflin Co., 1962.

Rosenthal, Robert, and Jacobson, Lenore. *Pygmalion in the Classroom.* New York: Holt, Rinehart & Winston, 1968.

Shepard, Paul, and McKinley, Daniel. *The Subversive Science.* Boston: Houghton Mifflin Co., 1968.

Stein, Maurice; Vidich, Arthur J.; and White, David Manning; eds. *Identity and Anxiety.* Glencoe, Ill.: Free Press, 1960.

Stent, Gunther S. "That Was the Molecular Biology That Was." *Science* 160 (1968): 390-95.

Whitehead, Alfred North. *The Aims of Education.* New York: Mentor Books, 1949.

The Beginning Teacher
of College Mathematics

R. L. WILDER

THE CULTURAL POSITION OF MATHEMATICS

One of the most important attributes that the new teacher of college mathematics should have acquired (in addition to the ability to handle the subject matter he is to teach) is knowledge of the general character of mathematics and its place in our culture. Some of the poorest teaching of mathematics is traceable to the instructor's treating his subject as though it had no connection with anything beyond its own confines.

This does not mean that it is sufficient for the instructor to bring in "applications" (something which may be quite difficult, since the students in the usual elementary college course have a diversity of ends in view). Rather, it means showing the relationships to those things that form part of man's common experience, such as the humanities, especially languages and philosophy. It includes, also, a general knowledge of the origins and intrinsic meanings of the topics covered. Mathematical "laws" (as the "laws of arithmetic") were not revealed to a Moses and handed down to the academic world. They are a human construction that evolved like any other aspect of human behavior; and although the rigid departmental structure of today's colleges seems to set mathematics firmly apart, the lines of separation from the other sciences and humanities are artificial.

If the new teacher has not himself been taught in such a way as to have already acquired such knowledge, it is not necessary that he take courses in history of mathematics or in philosophy of mathematics as a remedy for his deficiency. Indeed, these courses may not be taught in such a way as to provide the desired information. He may do better simply browsing among the books and articles that give explicit attention to these matters; for example, E. T. Bell, *The Development of Mathematics;* Morris Kline, *Mathematics in Western Culture;* and R. L. Wilder, *Evolution of Mathematical Concepts.* Throughout most of its history, mathematics was treated as one of the liberal arts, needing no justification by what are today called applications. It

Dr. Wilder is emeritus professor of mathematics, University of Michigan.

has been only in the last century or two, when pressures mounted for inclusion of many new fields in the college curriculum, that such justification was thought necessary. This is not to imply that the applications of mathematics are not worthwhile or important; they are. But they are only part of the cultural environment that has influenced and motivated mathematical evolution.

MATHEMATICS AS A LANGUAGE

It has become fashionable to call mathematics the language of science. A little analysis of this conception of mathematics is revealing. Consider the statement "Mathematics is a language," which, while less restrictive, carries similar connotations. Since languages are usually considered part of the humanities, this would make of mathematics a humanity—an idea for which there are other, more substantial grounds. Mathematics has many humanistic aspects that are not recognized so well today as they were during its liberal arts years. There was a time, during its early evolution, when mathematics was really part of the language of ordinary discourse. Moreover, if one analyzes the manner in which English is taught as a native language, one finds procedures quite similar to those employed in the teaching of early numerical and arithmetic facts. The parent uses such procedures intuitively, while the grade school teacher uses the methods he was taught during his professional training. But although the rules (grammatical in English, operational in arithmetic) and the problems posed may differ intrinsically, the analogy is very strong until the greater abstractions of the individual subjects are reached. In English courses, as traditionally developed, instruction becomes more literary at this stage, involving rules for writing fiction, nonfiction (especially exposition), and poetry, for instance. In mathematics, on the other hand, generalization (e.g., from arithmetic to algebra), consolidation (e.g., algebra with geometry), logical methods, and the increasing use and invention of symbolic apparatuses dominate. But until this stage is reached, a good argument can be given for the thesis that mathematics is a language.

Modern mathematics has grown and diversified to such an extent, however, that it can no longer be considered a language. By some natural scientists, as well as engineers who use many mathematical tools, mathematics might understandably be considered a language from an operational standpoint (although in modern physics, for example, many newly invented mathematical structures have come to play more of a conceptual than an operational role). Comparison can be made with the role of music in the life of a nonmusician. For the latter it is a form of entertainment, while to the professional musician, and especially to the composer, music has many conceptual forms as well as artistic and esthetic values that only the musically trained can appreciate.

MATHEMATICS AS AN ART

This brings us to the conception of mathematics as an art. For this idea there are stronger justifications than for the language concept of mathematics. Indeed, many mathematicians agree with this characterization of mathematics and consider that their creative work is essentially an artistic endeavor. Moreover, if one compares the psychological stages of creation—say, in the invention of a new mathematical structure, the development of a modern painting, and the composition of a symphony—he will find an almost identical progression in all three.

A SCIENCE OF STRUCTURES AND RELATIONS

Most mathematicians would probably agree today that mathematics is a science of structure and relations, which has evolved from the primitive forms of arithmetic and geometry under the influence of both external cultural and internal growth stresses. As such, it has acquired many humanistic qualities that qualify it both as a language and as an art, depending upon the uses made of it. Moreover, many have argued for seizing the opportunity to bring out, in mathematics teaching, those features of mathematics which can contribute to the inculcation of many of our cultural values.[1]

In a brief commentary such as this, it is impossible to give a complete justification of the statements made above. Consequently, a teacher not already familiar with them is urged to investigate them more thoroughly in the literature. He will inevitably have students, even among those whose future uses of mathematics will be purely technical, who would benefit by knowing something of the cultural aspects of mathematics. It is deplorable to allow a student to spend years in precollege and college mathematics without acquiring some knowledge of its place in and significance for man's culture.

TEACHING METHODS

Very likely the beginning teacher of mathematics at the college level will not have had any courses in teaching methods and will probably be guided, or at least strongly influenced, by the following factors: the methods used by the teachers who most impressed him during his studies, his own feelings about how he would like to have been taught the subjects that he is now teaching to others, and his intuition regarding the best way to get through to the particular students he is facing.

These factors are not independent, since each has an influence on

1. M. Richardson, "Mathematics and Intellectual Honesty."

the other two, depending upon the teacher's past experiences. For example, it is possible that no one of his own teachers made much of an impression; indeed, the first factor may have a somewhat negative effect, in that he may try to avoid the monotonous teaching to which he was subjected. If he has been so fortunate as to sit under an inspiring teacher, he may do well to consider adopting as many of the latter's methods as possible.

Since the new teacher is usually quite close to his own student days, he will probably remember how he was taught the subjects he is now teaching. Even after forty years of college teaching, this writer can still recall vividly the ways in which he was taught mathematics. In one of his courses, both the textbook and the instructor were poor, and from this experience he learned the importance of selecting suitable textbooks and avoiding certain teaching methods. From another instructor, the most inspiring of his college teachers, he learned the importance of an informal style that permits the class to interrupt for questions, to request repetitions, or to point out errors the instructor has made (everyone makes errors); and he learned the importance of cultivating a capacity for sensing, from students' attitudes, whether the class is finding the subject under discussion interesting. It appears that only experience, through contacts with other people, can develop this capacity. If, in one's social contacts, he has developed the habit of watching the reactions of others to his words, then he will likely extend this habit to his teaching. For he will have built up an intuitive awareness, through such contacts, of his impact upon his listeners' receptive faculties.

One should never forget that teaching unaccompanied by students' learning is hardly deserving of being called teaching. This fact seems to be overlooked in much of the discussion of what constitutes "good" teaching. The responsibility in the teaching process is as much the student's as the teacher's, and it may be a good idea now and then to remind the student tactfully of this fact. It would be interesting to know how much of the current student agitation for more inspiring teaching takes this into account. The person who teaches a subject to himself learns automatically, but many college students fail to understand that, as Plutarch said, "The mind is not a vessel to be filled, but a fire to be kindled." It is the teacher's task to kindle this fire.

GUIDELINES FOR TEACHING

On the basis of his many years of college teaching, this writer has found that the following principles, or guidelines, are of basic importance to the teacher of college mathematics.

1. *Never introduce a new concept without first motivating it.* Many

textbooks observe this rule, but wherever a textbook fails to do so, the teacher should use his lecture time to provide for the proper motivation.

A good example is found in teaching the mathematical induction principle. If the principle is stated in full, then explained, and then demonstrated as a method of proof, the teacher may expect the average student to be frustrated and to come up with questions such as, How can I find the $(n+1)$st term? that have nothing to do with the principle intrinsically. Instead of proceeding in this way, the teacher should *make use of what the student already knows*—in this case, how to count with the natural numbers. From this knowledge he can be led to discover the mathematical induction principle for himself, in the process he will develop an intuitive feeling for it, and he will then have little difficulty applying it.[2]

The real challenge comes when the teacher cannot readily recall an experience, such as knowledge of counting, common to all his students upon which to rely. In a "scientifically" planned curriculum, embracing both elementary- and secondary-school curricula and arranged with a view to anticipating future topics to be handled in their proper places, the teacher should have no difficulty. In its evolution mathematics grew through the creation of concepts for which already-known concepts provided a motivation. The new elementary-school curricula of today usually introduce intuitive geometric notions, so that when the student begins to study geometry seriously, he is better prepared with material upon which the teacher can build. Nevertheless, even with the best-designed curricula, situations will occur where the teacher must himself build up an adequate motivational background in the students, and this can tax his ingenuity severely. The challenge may prove exciting, however.

2. *Be honest.* One should never pretend knowledge of something that he does not really know. It is dangerous to do so; moreover, a class will usually respect and sympathize with a teacher who admits that he does not know the answer to a question and explains why. Indeed, such an event can often be turned to benefit if one encourages the student to find (or preferably, helps him find) the answer. This may build initiative in the students, and this initiative will in turn help to create interest.

There is an exception to this principle, and this relates to a pedagogical trick. It is sometimes advantageous for the teacher to pretend that he does not know the answer to a question in order to influence the class to help him work out the answer. Someone in the class may suspect the truth but, if so, will usually recognize the psychological

2. R. L. Wilder, "The Role of Intuition."

aspect so that no harm will result. Indeed, it will likely happen that when the teacher really does not know the answer, the class will credit him with knowing it, under the impression that he is using the trick.

3. *Do not overprepare.* The instructor should, of course, prepare topics that are to be taken up in class. On the other hand, overpreparation in the teaching of mathematics may lead to dull lecturing and to class interruptions, which may prove disruptive to a new teacher. Today's more aggressive student is very likely to reject being "lectured at" and to want the right to join in the discussion of a topic. Preparation should consist chiefly of refreshing one's knowledge of a topic.

But in presenting the topic in class one should stimulate the class to participate as much as possible in its development. Above all, the teacher should not state a theorem and at once give an elegant proof of it. First he should motivate the theorem by raising questions that the theorem to be stated is supposed to settle, then help the class to "discover" the theorem. Only then should the proof be worked out. Notice the words *worked out*. It is well known that first proofs of a theorem are usually clumsy; only later are elegant proofs found—this is true even of the work of the best research mathematicians. After a valid proof has been worked out in class, it is permissible for the instructor to give the most elegant proof known to him—after explaining, however, that the first, clumsier proof was quite the natural thing to find and not an indication of the class's inferiority. If the end of the class hour is so near as not to permit time to work out a proof, then the teacher might be wise to defer it to the next class hour, at the same time encouraging the class to think over the theorem and its implications and to consider how one might go about finding a proof. Sometimes a student will have a proof at the next class meeting.

4. *Do not be afraid to follow up a diversionary topic if it is brought up by the students.* If this principle is not observed, the students may become antagonistic both to the subject matter and to the instructor. There are exceptions, of course. If the topic brought up is too special and not likely to be of general class interest, then it is just as well to tell the questioner that he may discuss it with the teacher outside of class (and explain why). Or if the topic will more logically be taken up later, the teacher may explain that to the class.

Many courses, particularly at the freshman and sophomore levels, are supposed to cover a specified list of topics. With a little ingenuity, however, this can be done even though digressions are allowed. In some departments, the beginning instructor may be given a schedule to be followed, in which each topic is allowed a certain number of hours and the order of the topics is rigidly outlined. This practice not only is pedagogically bad but also ignores differences between both classes and instructors. Usually the purpose is to make the instructor keep up-to-date as well as to allow for uniform examinations in all sections of a course at specified periods (although the schedule is usually handed to the instructor under the guise of "helping him"!). The worst feature of this practice is that it ignores the maxim Better to do a few things well than many things badly. Differences in classes inevitably make it preferable to be flexible in allotting time to topics.

5. *Beware of lapsing into drill methods.* In the terminology of Professor Axelrod's article, don't be a type-A teacher. Mathematics is one of the subjects easiest to teach badly, since it is so symbolically oriented that it tends to allow what the writer calls *symbolic-reflex* teaching.[3] This is the kind of teaching one uses for "dumb" animals; the animal has no inkling of the conceptual aspects of a symbol—he merely learns to react to the symbol in a way that avoids disapproval or pain. But human beings can use symbols creatively; they *assign* the meanings to the symbols—something which, so far as has ever been ascertained, no animal other than man can do. (The statement applies to college teaching, of course, not to teaching a child just being introduced to language.) Consequently, one should teach in such a way as to encourage *symbolic initiative.* Usually the person who "hates math," or who "learns" proofs (a common error for the student of geometry) has been the victim of symbolic-reflex teaching.

Frequently it is stated that "mathematics is an activity; mathematics is *doing* mathematics." This has much truth in it when properly interpreted. It does not mean drill, except insofar as manipulative skill must be acquired as in playing the piano. The best pianist from the standpoint of technique may be rated poorly as a musician. Unless combined with exceptional interpretative skill and conception, faultless manipulation of difficult passages of music is not impressive. So, too, in mathematics. The ability to compute is not, as a rule, indicative of mathematical competence; some of the best mathematicians have been wretched computers. Manipulative skill cannot be ignored in such a highly symbolic subject as mathematics, and, indeed, it must be acquired; but it is a means to an end, and it is the end that is important. (Professor Boulding's remarks under his query seven, as well as his remarks under query six, are apropos in this connection.) It is to be hoped that some of the new programming and computer methods may take over most of the teaching of manipulative skills, leaving class time for background (motivational) and conceptual aspects of mathematics.

6. *Maintain enthusiasm for mathematics.* For one who has re-

3. R. L. Wilder, "The Cultural Basis of Mathematics."

search interests, this should be no problem. One must be careful, of course, not to allow research time to impinge on time that should be devoted to teaching tasks. Mathematicians have a debt to their successors and to society to pass on the torch of learning they have been handed. Moreover, every research mathematician will agree with Professor Boulding's remark, "Every good teacher learns as he teaches." This is true not only in courses closely related to one's own special field of research, but to seemingly unrelated elementary courses. Some of the most unexpected bits of wisdom, which throw a new light on some mathematical topic (not necessarily the one being taught), will pop into one's mind either during his own search for the best mode of presenting a concept or during class discussions.

If one does not have research interests, there are still many ways to keep alive an enthusiasm for mathematics. One of these is browsing in the extensive literature, which is becoming available in the form of new expository books and articles.

Back numbers of such journals as the *American Mathematical Monthly* contain much expository material, as well as interesting teaching hints. *Mathematical Reviews,* in addition to carrying abstracts of articles in all branches of mathematics, covers new discoveries in history, logic, and philosophy of mathematics; the exciting discoveries that have been made in the last decade are all recorded in this journal. Attendance at professional meetings, such as those of the Mathematical Association of America, will well repay the effort and expense involved by affording opportunity for establishing contacts with others having interests similar to one's own and for hearing outstanding speakers. In his reading, the teacher should be alert to detect items of import for his own mathematical interests. He may find that he has a knack for introducing unusual and novel slants in some areas of his teaching and ultimately may be moved to incorporate some of these in either a journal article or a new textbook. There is always room for originality in mathematics at every level, and the excitement of fostering one's abilities in this direction can be a fine incentive to inspiring teaching.

7. *Be receptive to questions of a general nature.* One of the most disturbing questions for the beginning teacher is What good is this?— usually asked by a student who is determined not to waste time studying topics of no apparent use to him. Paradoxically, "this" is usually of fundamental importance for an understanding of what is to come later and often of significance to the entire development of the subject being taught. However, the student's idea of mathematics is usually as an algorithmic tool; anything of value must be something that would enable one to grind out a numerical "answer." But the student has a right to an explanation—today he may demand it! In such

situations the teacher's best defense is his own knowledge and appreciation of the position of the questioned topic in the overall development
of the subject. Moreover, the student is perhaps affording the instructor a golden opportunity, not only to get outside and take an appraising
look at the subject, but also to expand upon the relevance of mathematics to our culture. This is an incidental way in which the desires
of students to participate in the examination and structure of course
content, mentioned by Professor Shamos, may be satisfied. Since
mathematics, contrary to popular belief, is not an absolute science but
one which allows considerable arbitrariness in its content, it is not
so much bound by the statement "Opinion is less important than evidence" (see Shamos) as are the natural and social sciences. It therefore affords an excellent opportunity for student participation in course
content (as well as a challenge to the instructor to defend the choice
of topics in a course)—something which has increasingly become
common in graduate courses bordering on research frontiers.

8. *Make clear the role of definition in mathematics.* Much of what
one will be teaching will involve defining concepts. Some of these
concepts will already be part of the student's mental equipment, but
only in an intuitive sense. One of the teacher's tasks will be to make
use of this intuition while at the same time making clear why mathematicians nevertheless have to *define* concepts. (Compare guideline
1 above.) Explaining this to the student will go far toward explaining
the general nature of mathematics.

9. *Get to know students individually as much as possible.* This has
become more difficult as the number of students has increased and
compelled colleges to resort to large sections and to the use of assistants.
The more aggressive students see that they do get to know the teacher,
but unfortunately some who most need counsel will hesitate to seek it.
The latter students run the risk of extreme frustration and of eventually dropping out. As the teacher becomes more experienced, he will
be better able to detect such students.

10. *Avoid teaching "at" the students.* Rather, consider learning-
teaching as a joint enterprise, in which the teacher's part is that of
guidance by a well-informed mentor (see guideline 3 above). Like any
mentor, a teacher is not infallible—and neither, for that matter, is
the subject he is teaching. Its limitations and arbitrariness are being
revealed at long last by modern research in logic and foundations.

Bibliography

Bell, E. T. *The Development of Mathematics.* New York: McGraw-Hill Book Co., 1945.

Benacerraf, Paul, and Putnam, Hilary, eds. *Philosophy of Mathematics.* Englewood Cliffs, N.J.: Prentice-Hall, 1964.

Boyer, Carl B. *A History of Mathematics.* New York: John Wiley & Sons, 1968.

Bronowski, Jacob. *Science and Human Values.* Rev. ed. New York: Harper & Row, Publishers, 1965 .

Court, N. A. *Mathematics in Fun and in Earnest.* New York: Dial Press, 1958.

Keyser, C. J. *The Human Worth of Rigorous Thinking.* New York: Columbia University Press, 1925.

Kline, Morris. *Mathematics in Western Culture.* New York: Oxford University Press, 1953.

Moise, E. E. "Activity and Motivation in Mathematics." *American Mathematical Monthly* 72 (1965): 407-12.

Ore, O. "Mathematics for Students of the Humanities." *American Mathematical Monthly* 51 (1944): 453-58.

Pólya, György. *Mathematical Discovery: On Understanding, Learning and Teaching Problem Solving.* 2 vols. New York: John Wiley & Sons, 1962-65.

Richardson, M. "Mathematics and Intellectual Honesty." *American Mathematical Monthly* 59 (1952): 73-78.

Waismann, Friedrich. *Introduction to Mathematical Thinking.* Translated by Theodore J. Benac. New York: Frederick Ungar Publishing Co., 1951.

Wilder, R. L. "The Cultural Basis of Mathematics." *Proceedings of the International Congress of Mathematicians* 1 (1950): 258-71.

———. *Evolution of Mathematical Concepts.* New York: John Wiley & Sons, 1968.

———. "Role of Intuition, The." *Science* 156 (1967): 605-10.

The Task of the Teacher in the Social Sciences

KENNETH E. BOULDING

TEACHING AS A SOCIAL SYSTEM

All human development, and one is tempted to add, all evolutionary development of any kind, is essentially a process of learning. Formal education, which might be defined as those learning processes which are assisted by a teacher, is only part of the total learning-process, and it must be evaluated in the light of the total process. This is particularly important in learning about social systems, because a great deal of what we know about social systems is learned outside of formal teaching. It is learned from members of the families in which we grow up, from playmates, schoolmates, comic books, television, and so on. We cannot become human without learning a good deal about the social system in which we find ourselves. Any formal teaching about social systems, therefore, must take as its background fairly complex images of society and of social relations, which are built up in the ordinary experience of life.

A good deal of this "folk knowledge" of social systems lies below the level of reflective thinking. We learn the appropriate behavior for different social groups, very much as we learn to walk, without much self-conscious theory of what we are doing. Folk knowledge of social systems, however, does express itself consciously in a body of "popular wisdom" in the form of aphorisms and proverbs. These represent a rich, though by no means systematic and consistent, body of folk wisdom about human relations. The very inconsistency—as expressed, for instance, in "Out of sight, out of mind" and "Absence makes the heart grow fonder"—may well reflect the richness, complexity, and inconsistency of the social system itself. Even the social sciences rely in part on the folk knowledge of the social scientists. Nevertheless, as the social scientists move toward maturity, they tend to diverge in their content more and more from the body of folk wisdom.

We have somewhat the same problem in the physical and biological

Dr. Boulding is professor of economics and program director, Institute of Behavioral Science, University of Colorado, and is a past-president, American Economic Association.

sciences. Here, however, the scientific knowledge is more remote from folk knowledge and can be built up from its own foundations. Thus the fact that what we learn in school about the solar system seems to contradict our daily experience does not bother us very much, for the contradiction can fairly easily be resolved. In social systems, however, the habit of generalizing from personal experience is so widespread that contradictions between "common sense" and the more sophisticated image of the world that comes out of scientific inquiry are not so easy to resolve. Nevertheless, it is the principal task of formal education in schools and colleges to expand the student's image of the world beyond his personal experience and to give him an image which encompasses the total system of the earth or even the universe.

The awkward mixture of folk and formal knowledge that constitutes even the sophisticated images of the social system may still give the teacher of the social sciences a certain advantage, in that the process of teaching and learning is itself part of the social system. Neither the physicist nor his students have ever been in—or even seen—an electron, nor has the biologist ever been in a cell, but both the teacher and the student of social systems have participated actively in many social systems of many different kinds. This potential advantage is by no means always exploited, for formal training in the social sciences does not always result in sensitivity in the interpretation of particular social systems in which the social scientist operates. Not only are the conclusions of research on the transfer of training very depressing, but the behavior of social scientists and their professional associations does not always reflect high standards of sophistication. Nevertheless, one hopes (perhaps foolishly) that the teacher in the social sciences should be in a particularly good situation to develop some concept of what he is doing as part of a larger social process. It is to be hoped, then, that he may perceive the teaching and learning process itself as essential to all social systems, as the process by which is transmitted and expanded that stock of knowledge on which all the other activities of a society are based. One hopes, again, the teacher of the social sciences, therefore, is perhaps in a better position than other teachers to visualize his impact. This impact is not merely the immediate product of the class that he is teaching but consists of what happens to his students, to himself, and to the social systems in which they participate for the rest of their lives as a result of their experiences in class. The teacher may then see that the main purpose of formal education is to facilitate the student's continuation of learning throughout his life. Education does this in a number of ways. It gives the student a vocabulary that will enable him to understand further communications and so continue his learning beyond the limits of the classroom. This vocabulary may include not only words but also mathematical and statistical symbols. It includes also conceptual contexts which should enable the student to fit further communications into a structure of increasing knowledge.

TEACHING AND LEARNING

The study of human learning is likely to be an extremely important area in the social sciences in the next generation and should produce marked changes in the practice of teaching. Teaching at all levels today is a skill based more on folk knowledge than on any explicit scientific knowledge of the learning process, and, while folk knowledge ns real knowledge in the sense that with its aid we have obviously succeeded in teaching people something over the centuries, it has limited horizons of development, which were almost certainly reached long ago. It is doubtful whether teaching today is much more effective in transmitting knowledge than it was in the schools of Athens. It is possible that we are on the edge of a substantial advance that should make teaching in this generation a peculiar challenge and delight. Thus if a teacher, especially in the field of the social sciences, can be aware that his classroom is a social system and that his teaching is also a form of research that may contribute to the advance of knowledge in this area, its significance is all the more enhanced.

We need to break down the view that teaching and research are totally unrelated activities. It is not only that teaching may be a form of research in human learning but also that the act of teaching forces a reexamination of the subject matter being taught, no matter what it is. Every good teacher learns as he teaches. This indeed is one of the miracles of teaching; it is not a form of exchange in which the teacher loses what the student gains but an extraordinary act of development in which, after the class, not only the student knows more but the teacher knows more. Teaching should also continually force a reexamination of the subject matter that is being taught, for the difficulties in transmitting subject matter from teacher to students come very frequently from a defect in the content of what the teacher is trying to transmit. It is much easier to believe nonsense than it is to teach it, and the very act of trying to teach nonsense becomes a self-correcting force.

EVALUATIVE FEEDBACK

One would hope to see considerable progress in the next generation in the integration of evaluation into the learning process. Little as we know about human learning, one of the principles that seems to be emerging is that evaluative feedback is a crucial element in all modifications of the image of the world. Evaluative feedback is crucial in folk learning. Thus, a child learns his native language largely by the selective responses of his parents and the people around him. When he starts babbling, he soon learns to select the sounds that are received with favorable responses, those on which, as it were, he gets an *A*, and to reject those which produce no response or unfavorable responses. Similarly, we learn to find our way around town because if our image of the world does not correspond to reality we get unfavorable evaluative feedback, often very quickly. If we go to the grocery store and it has moved, our disappointment produces a rapid learning process. Similarly, we learn who are our friends and enemies, we learn that immediate responses are not always wise ones, and we learn what gets us into trouble and what does not. The method of science, likewise, is essentially the method of organized evaluative feedback. It is only through the failure of predictions that science progresses.

It is only in the classroom that evaluation is sharply divorced from the learning process. The student does not learn easily why he has failed. Indeed, often he does not even get back his examination papers. The whole secret of programmed learning, insofar as there is one, is precisely to build evaluative feedback closely into the learning process, so that every time a student does anything it may be evaluated and the evaluation fed back to him. Programmed learning, however, is not the answer to all our problems. There are many learning processes, those which involve the structuring of complex images of the world, in which we have to learn to operate without much positive feedback or reinforcement for long periods. The mysterious processes by which the slow building up of vocabulary and grammar eventually leads to fluency in a language or by which little bits of learning eventually add up to mastery of a musical instrument are very little understood. Out of boredom or out of a sense of being insulted or out of a loss of personal dignity, programmed learning—if it is too picayune—may discourage people from learning. A good deal of the function of the teacher is to cheer students up, to encourage the discouraged, and to keep alive the students' sense of dignity and worth in a process that often destroys self-confidence and the sense of personal worth.

One hopes, therefore, that a substantial area of research in the effect of examinations, tests, grades, and other evaluative devices of the learning process will be developed in the next generation. We must evaluate evaluation itself as an element in a total social process, which is important not only in the learning process of the student who is being evaluated but also in the learning process of other people, both peers and superiors in the social matrix, with whom the student may be related.

All examinations and tests evaluate much more than knowledge of the subject matter. They also evaluate such things as a student's ability to solve puzzles, to write essays, to speak coherently, to organize material, to operate under stress, even the all-important ability to get away with things. If tests do not measure what they are supposed to measure, then decisions based on the results will be incorrect. The evaluation of the overall capacity of persons is a particularly delicate operation, and teachers should at least try to be conscious of what they are doing.

A peculiar difficulty in understanding the theory of the human learning-process is that we learn not only "facts"—that is, images of an external world—but also tastes, ethical values, and capacities for future learning. It is easy to see that our developing image grows toward "values" and that in some sense all learning is "wishful learning"; that is, we learn to see the world the way we do because it pays off. On the other hand, we learn about the payoffs themselves; for we do not come into the world like the birds, with a complete apparatus of genetically formed values. The values that we learn, furthermore, affect our capacity for further learning. If we learn that we cannot learn, or that we are "no good," we will not learn in the future. This is a system that defies the present skills of the systems analysts. It means, however, that we must be cautious about misinterpreting evaluative feedback, important as it is; for evaluative feedback, if it is poorly constructed, can easily destroy the capacity to learn. How do we distinguish between the kind of feedback which says, "I made a mistake, which I can correct," and the feedback which says, "I made a mistake, therefore I am no good, and I will continue to make mistakes." It may well be that the real difference between good and bad teaching lies precisely in differentiating between various kinds of evaluative feedback.

A NEED FOR RESEARCH

At the moment, the social sciences are very poorly organized to carry on research in the teaching-learning process. In graduate schools the gulf between research and teaching has gotten so wide that hardly any of the regular social science departments will tolerate a Ph.D. thesis in the teaching of its subject. Schools of education, unfortunately, often occupy the lowest position in prestige in the whole academic community. This is perhaps in part because of their use of the police power to force prospective teachers to take required courses and perhaps in part because of the general location of education in the grants sector of the economy, which tends to make it a field unremunerative by comparison, say, with law or engineering. Whatever the reason for this low status, it is nothing short of a disaster. Some persons believe that we might get along without good lawyers, who are engaged, after all, mainly in redistributing old property and resolving personal disputes. Some also believe that in these days we might even get along without good doctors, for the improvement in public health and the increase in the expectation in human life have been accomplished mainly by people outside the medical profession. If, however, we cannot transmit the knowledge that is in the heads of one generation into the heads of the next, society will inevitably decay. In any scale of social priorities, therefore, teaching should obviously stand very high. It is indeed a major challenge to the social sciences to find out why teaching and the study of teaching do not have a higher prestige and, perhaps, to recommend measures to correct this serious defect in our social system.

The first step toward a new science of learning and teaching would be, as it has been in many sciences, to develop a better "natural history." At the moment, each teacher is isolated in his classroom. Over the course of his life, he probably learns a good deal out of sheer experience. He learns that some things work and some things do not. If he is a good teacher, he will get a fair amount of feedback from his students and will modify his procedures accordingly. At the moment, however, there is practically no way by which this individual knowledge can be disseminated. The biological sciences owe a great debt to bird watching, even if bird watching is not strictly a science. Class watching, however, is regarded as a degrading business to be indulged in only by those who are supervising student teachers. In university teaching, especially, any outside intervention in the classroom is regarded as a deep threat to status, and resistance to it almost reaches proportions of paranoia.

There are, however, some hopeful signs. Some progress is being made by economists in reporting experiments in the teaching of economics, thanks in part to the Joint Committee on Economic Education and the Committee on Teaching of Economics of the American Economic Association. Similar progress is being made in other social sciences. The new *Journal of Economic Education* (vol. 1, no. 1, fall 1969) will be useful in opening up a new discourse. One possible means of freeing the teacher from the isolation of his classroom is the development of team teaching, even if this takes only the basic form of two colleagues teaching a single class. This perhaps is less threatening than having observers from outside, and if two people teach the same class, at least they will have something to talk about, and a conversation between them may attract others.

Outside Influences on Teaching

Three influences coming from outside the profession may affect the teaching process in the next generation, but exactly what the impact will be is hard to predict.

STUDENT UNREST

The first of these is the increasing student dissatisfaction and unrest. This is, in part, no doubt a consequence of the general disorders of our day and reflects what is perhaps a general unhappiness of the academic community with the draft, the rising power of the military, an "imperialistic" national image which seems more appropriate to an earlier period, and the increasing use of violence by the police. At least part of the student dissatisfaction, however, is directed specifically at the teaching and learning experiences to which they are subjected, and one must honestly confess their complaint is not wholly without foundation. A dean once told me that the one excuse he had never had a faculty member give is that he had to spend time preparing for his classes. The sheer economics—of the universities especially—gives strong marginal payoffs to research and writing and even to speaking outside the classroom, whereas the only reward for professors who spend a lot of time in teaching is, to quote W. S. Gilbert, "the gratifying feeling that our duty has been done." When we reflect how meager are the payoffs, we must realize it is a tribute, indeed, to the moral integrity of university faculties that teaching does not disintegrate even below its present level.

If student dissatisfaction can be channeled into some positive schemes for the improvement of teaching, it may well be one of the fortunate by-products of an otherwise rather calamitous era. Certainly the efforts at student evaluation of courses, which a good many universities now tolerate, could perhaps be linked up with a program of research and development in teaching that would make these evaluations less casual and more reliable. We are all aware, of course, that a popular teacher is not necessarily a good one and that many students are not able to identify their best teachers until they have been out of school for ten years or so. Still, popular teachers are frequently good ones, and there is probably some correlation between popularity and the capacity for inspiring students to learn.

EDUCATIONAL HARDWARE

The second outside effect on the teaching-learning process is likely to result from a massive attempt by manufacturers to introduce hardware—teaching machines, computer-assisted instruction, audiovisual aids and the like—into the teaching process. If the teaching profession remains passive in the face of this onslaught, it may well be disorganized by it, and the result will be disheartening, if not disastrous. We could easily see a parallel to the experience of the medical profession with commercial drug houses, the positive features of which are constantly being threatened by the incapacity of the medical profession to control its own inputs of information. It is not easy to see an answer to this problem. The teaching profession is not going to be able to control the research and development that are going into teaching devices. The only control, indeed, would come from a well-organized program in research in teaching that could act toward the teaching machines as, shall we say, the critics toward a play. In view of the reliance of the teaching profession, especially at the elementary and secondary levels, on compulsory schooling—and even on the use of the police power in the accreditation of teachers—a little commercial admixture into the occupation may not be wholly a bad thing, for if people can make money out of something honestly, there is continual pressure for improvement. Nevertheless, whatever beneficial effects the hardware revolution, if that is what it is going to be, can produce are likely to be much augmented if the teaching profession is organized to handle it and to criticize.

A great deal depends here on having a positive theory of teaching that can take (or leave) hardware in the light of testing, refining, and revising the theoretical structure. The great danger of hardware is that it tends to concentrate on specific and particular performances and behavior and by its very nature cannot be concerned with the total development of the individual. It is argued that hardware will relieve the teacher from burdensome and unnecessary duties and leave him free to concentrate on the great personal task of developing the total personality of the student. This sounds fine, but one has one's suspicions, and a nightmarish future in which the teacher becomes primarily an electronic repairman and the students all turn into well-trained rogues and clods is not inconceivable. It may be, of course, that the hardware will not be efficient enough to justify its cost. The teacher, as someone has said, is a nonlinear computer of enormous capacity produced initially by entirely unskilled labor, and the economics of biology in the long run may outrun the economics of mechanical and electrical engineering. Here, however, we must simply wait and see and be prepared for the unexpected.

CONTENT AND ORGANIZATION OF SOCIAL SCIENCES

The third, and perhaps in the long run the most important, effect on the teaching of social sciences is likely to come from the content and the organization of the social sciences. The change in the content of the social sciences as time goes on obviously affects what is taught. One is reminded of the old story about the alumnus who visited his old department and found that the questions that were being asked on the examinations were the same as those that he had answered a generation ago. He was reassured of progress, however, by the professor, who explained that while the questions might be the same, the answers were now different. Certainly in the last fifty years there has been a marked change in the answers. For instance, in economics the Keynesian system has triumphed, in psychology the instincts have been abandoned, in political science quantification is no longer a dirty word.

From the point of view of the teacher, perhaps one of the major questions of the next generation is whether the social sciences will exhibit any convergence or reorganization. The existing division into economics, political science, sociology, anthropology, psychology, and so on is the result of a long historical process with at least some random elements in it. Whatever may have been past justifications for the existing division, we should not necessarily assume that these will persist indefinitely. In fact, all social sciences are studying the same thing, that is, the total social system.

This might be called the "sociosphere" by analogy with the biosphere or the atmosphere. It consists of all three billion human beings; their inputs and outputs of commodities and information associated with them; the roles which they occupy and the organizations constructed out of these roles; the symbols, images, and knowledge embodied in their nervous systems; and so on. Social systems are differentiated fairly sharply from biological systems by the importance of information, symbols, and consciousness in them. There is a real difference in systems level between the study of the social system and, say, even the study of human physiology. The social sciences, however, are not divided from each other by differences in systems level, but by the fact that they abstract somewhat different elements and concentrate on different parts of the social system. Thus, economics concentrates on exchange and exchangeables and on how the social system is organized through exchange. It concentrates heavily on those organizations and institutions that are concerned primarily with exchange, such as banks, corporations, and public finance agencies. Political science concentrates primarily on institutions that are organized through legitimated threat, such as governments. Sociology deals primarily with integrative relationships and tends to take institutions that concentrate on community and solidarity—and their opposites—such as the family, the church, crime, the military, and so on. Anthropology, historically, has concentrated on the study of small societies and especially of primitive societies. Psychology concentrates on studies of the behavior of individual organisms; social psychology, on behavior of small groups.

The arbitrary nature of the existing divisions of the social sciences is reflected first in the fact that almost any attempt to characterize them will produce substantial protest from the practitioners. Thus, economists will protest that what they are really studying is the allocation of resources under conditions of scarcity. On the other hand, political scientists want to get into this one too and define political science as an authoritative allocation of resources through public institutions. Sociologists will complain that economists have no monopoly on the concept of exchange and that social exchange is an essential characteristic of sociological systems. Anthropology, at least in the guise of social anthropology, pushes its claim towards larger and larger societies. Another aspect of the arbitrariness of the present divisions is that the differences within the existing disciplines are probably greater than the differences between them. This is especially true of psychology, which is an extraordinary aggregation of almost unrelated studies close to physiology and ethology at one end and into clinical psychology and "literary psychoanalysis" at the other. It could be argued, indeed, that in the systems level there is a fundamental difference between the "micro" and the "macro" in virtually all the existing disciplines.

In defense of the existing structure of the social sciences, one can only say that each of the disciplines creates a subculture, the members of which can talk fairly easily to each other, but not easily to those in other disciplines. If, however, the existing disciplinary structure does not in fact represent the most useful mode of division, the development of these disciplinary subcultures is an all the more damning indictment. We can hardly take much satisfaction in the reflection that the training of social scientists has become so highly specialized that each field has tended to create a little world of discourse of its own with high protective tariffs against intrusions from other fields. In the universities especially, the fact that the major political power rests with the departments and the professions they represent means that attempts to teach a unified social science are regarded with suspicion or even with contempt. Each discipline tends to live within itself and to think that there is not much that it has to learn from others. The economist, for instance, is not trained to think of economics as simply a contribution to a larger system but tends to think of it as something completely self-contained and unrelated to other disciplines. A case perhaps can be made for this attitude at the graduate level, where the tricks of the trade have to be learned, but at the high school or undergraduate level, this intellectual isolationism can be disastrous. There is great need for teachers who can respect their own disciplines and at the same time give the student a sense of the totality out of which he can abstract some particular segment. An occupational disease of the academic is that of mistaking an abstraction for reality, and this is particularly dangerous in the social sciences.

A serious problem for teaching in the social sciences is created by the fact that the lower the grade level of the student, the more difficult the question of content. At the graduate level there is not much of a problem, as the student has to learn the current, detailed content of his own profession. At the level of freshman or sophomore courses, which are supposed to be more general, the problem of content is acute. It is a deplorable aspect of the American tradition in higher education that these lower-level courses are usually taught by younger faculty members, who are the most ill prepared to teach them. The German tradition, in which the elementary courses in the subject were usually taught by the senior professor, has much to recommend it, and universities should not be above using economic incentives to persuade senior members to teach elementary courses.

In the high schools and grade schools, the problem of content in the social sciences becomes all the more acute and, apart from some fine work like that of Lawrence Senesh, social science pays little attention to what should be taught in the lower grades. At the high school level, some attention is now being paid to the problem, but with practically no coordination among the different social scientists. What is desperately needed here is an elementary, general social science of adequate content, but there is literally no apparatus in the professions or in the schools for producing one. If anything, the interest of university people in the high schools is contributing to even further fractionation of social science. Economists are pushing economics, sociologists are pushing sociology, and so on, with potentially disastrous results.

A word should be said here for geography and history, each of which has an ambiguous, but highly important, relation to the social sciences. Geography has a strong claim to being the principal integrator of all the sciences, insofar as it studies the earth as a total system. The fact that it is already well-established in the lower schools suggests that it could play a key role in introducing concepts of the social system in the first twelve grades. Unfortunately, it suffers as a discipline from some lack of organized contact with the social sciences and also from a quite unwarranted feeling of inferiority. It can provide an important link between the social sciences and the biological and physical sciences, and one can visualize a curriculum in which all the sciences are organized in an essentially geographical setting.

History as a discipline straddles the social sciences and the humanities and should indeed provide an important link between them. The historical record, in the larger sense, is the raw material from which all science must come, and the record of human history and experience is the great mine of information from which the precious metals of understanding have to be extracted by an enormous process of orderly sifting and rejection of information. The historian's skill in appraising, sifting, condensing, and interpreting the deposits of the historical record is an essential part of the general search for stable patterns and interpretative theories. Here again, if social science is to be taught in the first twelve grades, a great deal of the teaching must be done in the name of history, a kind of history which creates real understanding of both the necessities and the accidents of the total social process. The sociosphere, after all, is a four-dimensional body with three dimensions of space and one of time. The historian is absolutely necessary to the filling out of the fourth dimension. The social scientists, however, can perform a crucial role in discovering the patterns within the "noise."

It is not easy to be optimistic about the progress, at least in the next generation, of the social sciences toward an integrated body of content. Nevertheless, if there is one element in the social system itself that will push us towards this seemingly utopian goal, it is the pressure of teaching and the pressure of teachers. We have already noted the impact of teaching on the content of what is taught. One would like to stir up a revolt of the teachers, and especially teachers below the graduate level, against the unsatisfactory nature of much of the content that they are expected to teach. Here again the need for a marriage of teaching and research in a single learning process has never been more clear.

THE SOCIAL SCIENCES AS A SENSITIVE AREA

One of the most critical problems facing the institutions and the practitioners of formal education is the relationship of these institutions and persons to the world around them, which largely pays for them and yet is apt to be dominated by a folk culture with images of the world very different from those which prevail within the walls of the school or college. This problem is perhaps more nearly acute today than at any other time in human history, simply because we are in an enormous transition in the state of the human race, largely as a result of formal education and its offshoots in science. Under these circumstances, the tension between the values and images of the academic and scholastic community and those of the outside world is likely to be severe. The physical sciences and the biological sciences had to fight this battle somewhat earlier. On the whole, they won it. No longer does the outside world consider a school teaching Copernican astronomy or Einsteinian physics or Darwinian evolution to be a threat, though we sometimes forget that this was a long, hard battle and that until a recent court decision there were still two states where the teaching of evolution was formally, if ineffectually, prohibited by law. Nowhere in formal education does anybody have to teach that the earth is flat. In the social sciences, however, the equivalent of the flat-earth image is still very powerful, and people who hold such views are naturally upset by the heretical views which their children bring home from school. The kind of sophisticated images that are involved in such things as the Keynesian economics, the modern theory of the international system, or the sociology of education or religion would create tensions with less sophisticated counterparts even if no value problems were involved. All this puts the teacher of the social sciences into a peculiarly difficult position and makes the ethical problems of teaching, which arise in all disciplines, acute.

The social sciences thus occupy an area that is much more sensitive than that of the physical or biological sciences. They deal with matters that are controversial, political, and of great importance to people in their daily economic, political, and social lives. At many points the findings and concepts of the social sciences tend to run counter to those of the folk culture, and it is not surprising that opposition is aroused. These matters cannot be ignored by the teacher, for in the first place they are an essential part of the social system that he studies and teaches, and in the second place his students quite rightly come to the social sciences in the hope of finding light in the dark political, social, economic, and ethical controversies of their own day. At least part of the student dissatisfaction in universities, which is showing some signs of getting into the high schools, arises from the conviction that students are not receiving the help they need in finding what is relevant to their own problems, both personal and political. Students feel a strong need to know more about such problems as the draft, the war, urban decay, poverty, racial discrimination, taxation and public expenditure. The teacher of the social sciences simply cannot pretend that these problems do not exist. Neither can he claim that the social sciences give simple and unequivocal answers to them.

DIFFERING VALUE SYSTEMS

The problem arises partly, as we have seen, because the value system of the scientific and academic communities tends to be different from that of the world around them. Science first arose in a small European subculture, which developed an unusual value system putting a high value on curiosity, openness, and veracity and a low value on any authority but that of evidence. These values are not characteristic of many folk cultures or even of many fairly well developed political cultures. They are not characteristic, for instance, of the international system, where secrecy rather than openness is the rule, power is more highly valued than truth, and veracity is valued only if it serves the purposes of power. In the business community, in the labor movement, and even in the church, the system of ethical priorities may differ in quite important respects from the ethical system of science. The teacher of the social sciences especially must be self-conscious of these matters and is under an almost Hippocratic obligation to encourage the growth of a similar self-consciousness in students. Self-consciousness in any shape, however, may be the enemy of certain folk values. I recall, for instance, being in the company of some anthropologists on the Fourth of July when the fireworks were starting in the town square and overhearing one say to another, "Let's go down and see the tribal rites." A good, simple-minded patriot might well be scandalized at hearing his sacred observances compared to tribal rites. The acids of self-consciousness, however, are always eating away at traditional legitimacies, and as one of the principal objects of the social sciences is to create social self-consciousness, the threat to ancient legitimacies, which this postulates, may be quite real.

SOCIAL SCIENCES AND ETHICS

One of the most delicate and important problems in social science is its relation to ethical principles and practices. There is little agreement, indeed, on the nature of its responsibility for them. There are those who argue that this is something that should be left entirely to the folk culture, that formal education has no responsibility for the development of ethical principles for the inculcation of ethical conduct, and that the social sciences have no more responsibility for this than do any other fields. This view seems to me unrealistic. In the first place, it is virtually impossible to change the "image of fact" in the mind of a person without at the same time changing his image of value. Our evaluations of the world and our preferences depend on our total view of what the world is like. If a student learns in the family that the earth is flat, we cannot teach him in school that the earth is round without creating a whole set of readjustments of his value system, for if he believes his school teacher he will have to adjust to the fact that his parents are in error. He will have less respect for the opinions of his parents, whatever respect he may have for their persons, and his whole value system is very likely to take a subtle shift, for he is very likely to have less respect for his family's preferences in general. The great debate about indoctrination, which has been going on in educational circles for two generations, cannot be resolved by pretending that we can have a value-free education.

A further problem arises, as we have noted above, because science itself has a strong ethical base and cannot exist without strong ethical principles, which may easily run into conflict with the ethical principles of the culture around it. Any kind of epistemological process involves some kind of payoff. Human learning, indeed, is inconceivable without a set of preferences. Wherever there is a set of preferences that is assumed to have some sort of universal validity, or at least to go beyond those tastes that are purely personal and about which there is supposed to be no disputing, an ethical system is involved. Knowledge without ethics, and education without ethics, are therefore inconceivable. The principle that scientists and educators simply take their ethical systems from the community around them is untenable. This forces the question: Does the social scientist, as representing that segment of the intellectual, scientific, and educational community that specializes in the study of social systems, have a special responsibility for the formulation, or even the propagation, of ethical principles that are appropriate for the educational enterprise? This is a view which most social scientists would reject, probably on the grounds that their concern is only with what is, not with what ought to be. This, however, assumes a naive epistemology. We cannot get to know things simply by comparing our images with reality, for as Hume pointed out a long time ago, this cannot be done; images can only be compared with images. The scientific method is not a method of discovering truth. It is a method for organizing feedback from error and so, if hopes are realized, for approaching truth by progressively eliminating error. The proposition that we should eliminate error, however, is an ethical proposition, one indeed which can even be called into question; for the proposition that under some circumstances ignorance may be bliss is not one that can be disproved easily, if at all.

Furthermore, the society's ethical principles profoundly affect its preferences, its decisions, its behavior, and hence its dynamic course. Even the social scientist who eschews admonition and exhortation, or thinks he does, cannot avoid studying the impact of the ethical principles on society, for these are an essential part of his subject matter. What is more, insofar as he is interested in teaching and learning as a social system, he should have a special interest in the ethical principles that are appropriate to this social system because he is a participant in it. If he believes in self-improvement and in improving his own performance as a teacher, he should be willing to scrutinize his own behavior, not only in the light of the general folk ethic to which he adheres, but in the light of his image as a social scientist studying the teaching-learning process.

QUERIES FOR SELF-ANALYSIS

The Quakers have developed an ingenious method of collective ethical analysis in their *queries,* a set of loaded questions intended in these days primarily for self-examination but also continually revised to meet the consensus of the group. Thus, the query has a certain advantage over the *commandment,* in that even the query itself may be questioned. Hence, it leads to ethical analysis rather than to dogma. The following queries for teachers are therefore intended to provoke ethical analysis, and they are, of course, relevant to all teachers. Social scientists, however, may have a peculiar responsibility for seeking further knowledge about the implied social system.

1. Do I abuse my position of superior status to the student by treating him as a moral or social inferior?

The problem of the relevance of the status structure of the classroom, or more generally the problem of the teacher-student relationship, to success in the teaching-learning process is one that needs much further study. To a certain extent the teacher-student relationship, by its very nature, is hierarchical, in that a teacher is supposed to know more than a student or at least he is supposed to teach the student more than the student teaches him. In an unbalanced exchange of this kind, hierarchy always arises. Furthermore, in the organization of education the teacher is usually in a superior position in the threat system. He can threaten a student with failure as a student much more effectively than the student can threaten him with failure as a teacher. He grades the student, the student does not usually grade him. This is the kind of situation in which arises the possibility of abuse. We need to know much more about the effect of exploitation of status on the learning process. We need to know more, for instance, about the effects of bullying and sarcasm in blocking learning. On the other hand, it is also possible that too much emphasis on equality of status between the teacher and the student, by making the student inattentive or disrespectful and unwilling to accept what the teacher has to say, may also diminish the effectiveness of the learning process. One of the principal research problems here is the measurement and detection of these status attitudes. At the moment they are never clearly defined in the evaluation of the teacher, and because of this many teachers who do enormous damage to the learning process may be employed.

2. Am I careful to avoid using my authority to force factual accep-

tance of propositions which may be only opinion or hypothesis? Do I tolerate honest disagreement? Would I be pleased if I were ever proved to be wrong by a student?

This question is closely related to the first. The authority of the teacher, because he is also the examiner or judge, is dangerously great, and the teacher may be unwilling to accept challenge to his authority, either from his students or from the world around him. It is part of the myth of science that authority comes only from the "real world," not from authoritative persons, past or present. It is not easy for any kind of scientist to convey this in the classroom where the status symbols—the desk, the podium, the blackboard—all reinforce the authority of the teacher rather than the authority of the subject matter itself. One could visualize some interesting experimental work in this field with a view to finding out what kind of teaching produces the scientific ethic and what kind produces the authoritarian ethic.

3. Do I express my overt or covert hostility to my students in my teaching? Am I irritated by student failure, or am I quick to detect and encourage growth in knowledge and understanding, however slow or imperfect?

This query raises the question of the personality of the teacher, rather than of his attitude toward status, although the two are clearly related, for hostile people have a strong tendency to seek authoritarian status. It would be interesting to know whether teaching attracts more hostile personalities than other occupations. We might well find that teachers are sharply bimodal, that some are attracted into the profession because they find the transmission of knowledge pleasurable. These people are likely to be friendly, rather than hostile, toward the student. Others, however, may enter the profession because they have failed elsewhere. One recalls Bernard Shaw's unkind crack "Those who can, do. Those who cannot, teach." Teachers who are frustrated executives or politicians are very likely to work out their frustrations and hostilities on the students, and this may be damaging to the learning process. Here again, an instrument which would detect this kind of hostility and frustration would be of great value, for the teacher who is both hostile and authoritarian may be enormously damaging.

4. Am I myself interested in the subject matter that I am teaching? Do I enjoy learning more about it, and do I carry over to the student my own enthusiasm for the subject?

There is a widespread belief that a teacher's enthusiasm for his subject can compensate for a good many deficiencies in his technique. A famous example of this was John R. Commons of the University of Wisconsin, who is reported to have been a very poor lecturer; yet he inspired a whole generation of students who were active, for instance, in developing the New Deal and who in many ways changed the face of America. The negative proposition is probably more easily demonstrated than the positive one; certainly the teacher who is bored with his own subject makes life miserable for his students as well as for himself. For this reason, there is much to be said for rotating courses among teachers, so that nobody teaches the same course for too long.

5. Do I convey to my students both the setting and the significance of my subject matter, so that it appears neither isolated nor irrelevant?

This query is closely related to the previous one, though it covers a slightly different point. A teacher may often be enthusiastic about his own particular speciality, without himself appreciating adequately where it stands in the great republic of learning and what its broad significance may be. There is a certain division of opinion here between those who favor orderly presentation of subject matter and those who believe that the main function of the teacher is to digress, assuming that the textbook is usually orderly enough and that the function of the teacher is to introduce a little creative disorder by showing the student that no subject is as tidy as it seems.

6. Do I convey to the student the necessity for intellectual discipline and a sense of the need for hard work on difficult intellectual tasks if the practical problems of our society are to be solved?

This query should perhaps be particularly addressed to idealistic teachers who have idealistic students. Good will is a complement, not a substitute, for good knowledge. Likewise, euphoria is a very poor substitute for truth. While dullness has a strong claim to being considered as the most deadly sin of the teacher, excitement in itself is not always a virtue, for it may distract people from doing the hard, slogging work that is always necessary for the mastery of a difficult subject. There is a delicate problem of balance here. The teacher, especially in the social sciences, can easily discourage the idealist too greatly by pointing out the extraordinary difficulties that lie in the way of good social change. Like Hamlet, we need to avoid being "sicklied o'er with the pale cast of thought." The teacher in the social sciences, especially, has to walk a difficult tightrope between the kind of despair and atrophy of the moral sense that sometimes comes from overintellectualization and the hyperactivity that can easily be destructive of those who are both morally aroused and proudly ignorant.

7. Do I convey to the student the importance of technical skill and, at the same time, leave him problem-oriented rather than technique-oriented, the master and not the servant of the skills which he has acquired?

This query, again, is closely related to the preceding one, but it is addressed to what is the particular vice of the social sciences, especially of economics. Techniques usually arise in response to problems, and certainly one needs to encourage the use of the best intellectual tools. On the other hand, techniques tend to have a certain life of their own and to become ends in themselves. This is particularly true of advanced statistical and mathematical techniques. Furthermore, the ability to use a technique and to develop technical skill becomes a point of professional pride and a measure of professional achievement. This is dangerous if it leads to an evaluation on the basis of ability to manipulate existing techniques, rather than from the point of view of ability to struggle with the "real world." The danger of technique-oriented education is that it creates what Veblen called "trained incapacity"— persons who are trained exclusively in techniques prefer to do only the things that can be done with the techniques that they have learned rather than to tackle jobs that may be more important but that are unresponsive to their existing tools, like a surgeon insisting on using his scalpel to dig away a snowdrift. The teacher often tends to underrate what he does not understand and overrate what he does understand, and it is hard for him to walk a tightrope between these two extremes.

8. Is my relation to other teachers one of cooperation in a great common task of transmitting and extending the knowledge structure of society, or am I jealous and suspicious of others? Am I conscious of my citizenship in the academic community? Do I insist on doing only those things that will lead to my personal advancement?

This query raises large and difficult issues. Advancement in the academic community rarely comes from good teaching. Still more rarely does it come from doing the necessary "menial" intellectual labor of the academic community. In the absence of an economic system that rewards good teaching directly there is great necessity for constant reiteration of the ethical principles of what constitutes good citizenship in the academic community. Communities, however, may be subject to "ethical strain" where the organization of the community, and especially of the reward structure, does not conform to real interests and productivities. Ethical strain is a much neglected area in the social sciences—indeed, the concept is hardly recognized. We are becoming intensely aware of it, however, in such problems as economic development, relations with government, and the power structure in general. Hypocrisy, subterfuge, and corruption are visible symptoms of ethical strain. The social sciences may perhaps make an important contribution to solving this problem by pointing out that the answer to ethical strain may not lie in stepping up the level of exhortation and preaching. It may lie, rather, in reorganizing the institutions and the payoffs of society itself. This is as true inside the academic community as it is outside it. It is one of the paradoxes of the social sciences, indeed, that whereas social science is used to study practically every tribe and every form of human organization and relationship, the one great unstudied area is the university itself, perhaps because it is too close to home. A much more serious social science study of educational organizations than we have had in the past should clearly be on the agenda for the future.

9. Do I have a proper sense of my own dignity as a teacher and researcher, and do I have an equivalent sense of the dignity of all those with whom I come in contact?

This query perhaps summarizes all the others. Unless the teacher has a sense of his own worth and of the importance of his task, he should be doing something else.

I am content to leave the matter at this point and to conclude with a personal testimony that for thirty-five years I have found teaching, with all its frustrations and difficulties, to be a very good life, and I expect the situation to continue in the future.

Bibliography on Economics

American Economic Review Proceedings, May 1961-68. Sessions on the teaching of economics.

Haley, B. F. "The Content of the Introductory Course." *American Economic Review Proceedings,* May 1962, pp. 474-82.

Knopf, K. A., and Stauss, J. H., eds. *The Teaching of Elementary Economics.* New York: Holt, Rinehart & Winston, 1960.

Lumsden, Keith G. *New Developments in the Teaching of Economics.* Englewood Cliffs, N.J.: Prentice-Hall, 1967.

Taylor, Horace, ed. "The Teaching of Undergraduate Economics." Report of the Committee on the Undergraduate Teaching of Economics and the Training of Economists. *American Economic Review* supplement, December 1950.

The Teaching
of Psychology

ROBERT B. MACLEOD

This chapter might be subtitled "Questions addressed to a beginning teacher of psychology." And if it were, my first word of advice would be: Be coolly skeptical about questions raised by a member of the older generation and especially about his answers. The beginning teacher should begin by thinking for himself; if he does not, he may find it difficult at a later date to assert his independence. This generation of students is calling for a thoughtful reappraisal of the whole meaning of higher education. In spite of occasional excesses, it is a healthy movement. To the young teacher, who is still close to his own student experience, it should be a challenge to do a bit of radical thinking, not only about the formal organization of higher education but also about its implicit philosophy. There may, it is true, be some residual wisdom in our tradition, but it should not be accepted without careful examination.

Actually, I am not worried about the young teacher's being too radical; I am worried about his being too conservative. There is little in the graduate training of prospective college teachers that invites a fresh approach to higher education. The following questions are directed to the teacher of psychology, but they might be directed to the teacher of any subject.

1. What is your purpose in teaching psychology?
2. What kind of psychology are you teaching?
3. To whom are you teaching it?
4. How are you teaching it?
5. How are you preparing yourself to teach it?

Most of these questions are raised in other chapters by Kenneth Boulding and Stanford Ericksen. Here they are pointed especially toward the introductory course in psychology. My own biases will be clear, and these can be readily discounted.

HISTORICAL NOTE

Psychology in one form or other has been in the curriculum since the beginning of the American college. Until the latter part of the

---

Dr. MacLeod is professor of psychology, Cornell University.

nineteenth century it was taught by philosophers as a discipline ancillary to metaphysics, epistemology, logic, and ethics. For philosophical psychology at its best, read William James's *Principles of Psychology* (1890), probably the best single book on psychology ever written in English. James examines the classic problems of psychology as problems to be solved through careful observation and clear thinking, using the methods of the sciences where these are relevant, but never hesitating to challenge the assumptions both of the sciences and of traditional philosophy and never disparaging the practical problems of everyday living.

The influence of James was tremendous. Generations of students revered him and studied his textbook, but the pattern of subsequent psychology was dictated by antiphilosophical movements. The first was the "new psychology" of the laboratory, heralded by Wilhelm Wundt. It was based on the method of analytic introspection and attempted to correlate elementary states and processes of consciousness with antecedent and concomitant physical and physiological conditions. Around the turn of the century there was a steady trickle of German-trained psychologists, the most notable of whom was E. B. Titchener, dedicated to the thesis that psychology could be established as an independent experimental science. Laboratories were founded in the leading universities, psychology demanded and achieved its independence from philosophy, and a standard psychological curriculum began to be recognized. The beginning teacher of psychology will find a classic model in Titchener's *Textbook of Psychology*.

The second movement was represented by a wave of biologically oriented psychologists who were impatient with introspective analysis and wanted to establish psychology as an objective science of behavior. The prime mover was probably C. Lloyd Morgan, the Welsh biologist, but in this country the great pioneer was E. L. Thorndike and the most vocal expositor was John B. Watson. The movement, loosely known as *behaviorism* but more properly designated *stimulus-response* (S-R) *psychology*, seems to have won the battle against analytic introspectionism. The language of stimulus-response lends itself readily to the conception of man as an adjusting organism. Actually both movements have much in common. Together they represent the ideal of psychology as one of the natural sciences, and they provide the core of the "basic psychology" which is found in virtually every curriculum in the country.

The pioneers soon began to discover that their psychology could not be kept indefinitely within the confines of the laboratory. The problems of society, particularly in the fields of education, industry, and medicine, insistently demanded that psychological principles and methods be practically applied. The requirements of two world wars dramatized these needs, first for the development of psychological tests and second for the development of clinical procedures. There consequently came into being, particularly after World War II, a significant and well-organized profession of psychology, which in turn demanded that the teachers in the colleges should train their students for professional practice. The demand for professional preparation itself opened up for scientific investigation areas of human behavior that had not been explored by the traditional experimentalists.

In recent years the field of psychology has been extended still further from man as an adjusting organism to man as a member of society, and psychologists have been finding new and stimulating colleagues among anthropologists, sociologists, economists, political scientists, and even historians.

Thus we see that psychology, without having discarded its classic problems, has been reaching out into a multitude of fields, each of which involves a broadening of its subject matter and often requires a revision of its methods. One might conclude that psychology is now in a state of chaos. Certainly its public image has become quite blurred; one man's conception of psychology may be almost wholly different from that of someone else. Whether or not psychologists can find a simple definition of their subject that is not so comprehensive as to be meaningless, the beginning teacher of psychology must realize that he will be addressing students with widely divergent conceptions of what it is they are going to be studying.

THE TEACHER

The teacher might, at one extreme, choose to be an eclectic and give a little bit about all possible topics that are considered to be psychological; at the other extreme he might decide to give his own interpretation of psychology and discard everything else as irrelevant. Both extreme approaches are probably wrong; the teacher must find some sort of middle ground. Whatever his final compromise, the teacher owes it both to himself and to his students to be fully aware of what he is doing. A merely eclectic approach without evaluation provides little stimulation; indoctrination without consideration of alternatives is equally bad. The good teacher will make his own biases explicit, but before he can do this he must become aware of them.

Hence the following questions. Every one of these involves every other, but there may be some value in asking them separately.

1. What is your purpose in teaching psychology?

Let us discard as irrelevant and unworthy such answers to the question as: I am trying to earn a living; I like the comfort and freedom of the academic world, and to achieve this sort of life I must do a minimum of teaching. Or: I want to become a dean or a president, and teaching is the first step on the ladder. Some other answers, which at first glance seem to be a little more reasonable, should be examined critically: I am a junior member of the department of psychology; I want to build the enrollment in our courses, to enlist more majors, to send more students to good graduate schools. Or: Since our best students go on to graduate school, I am preparing them to do well on the Graduate Record Examination and to meet the other graduate school requirements. Such answers as these are also unworthy.

As a teacher of psychology, you are a member of the faculty of an institution dedicated to the education of the next generation. You believe that your subject can make an important contribution to the education of students, but your final criterion is the education of the student, not the welfare of your particular department or specialty. This means that as a teacher of psychology you must think of yourself first as a member of a larger team of teachers, all of whom are concerned primarily with the education of students. This means that you must think through for yourself a philosophy of education, and in the context of this philosophy you must assess the educational values of the psychology you are teaching.

2. What kind of psychology are you teaching?

One answer to that question might be: A vast amount of information labeled psychology is regularly published in books and periodicals. Such information is part of our culture, and my duty as a teacher is to make the next generation acquainted with it.

There is something to be said for this approach, and certainly it is supported by the most popular of the contemporary textbooks. The survey course, which must be constantly revised to be up-to-date, has a noble history. In the days of Chicago's A. J. Carlson, it set a pattern of scholarship for teachers throughout the country. At its best it has provided exciting glimpses of science and scholarship at the frontier. At its worst—and the worst is probably to be found in the social sciences—it has served merely to differentiate between what is "in" and what is "old hat." For psychology this approach can be self-destructive. The literature of contemporary psychology is stuffed with commentaries, speculations, and reports of investigations that will not survive for even a decade. These must, of course, be combed by an expert for residual facts and insight, but to require of the student a knowledge of acquaintance with the trivia of contemporary psychological writing is not only to waste the student's time but to hamper his education.

My view—and it may be registered as a prejudice—is that any psychology worth teaching is a psychology centered on problems that have persisted since the beginning of recorded history, problems connected with man's conception of himself and of his relation to the world about him. Ultimately these are problems of philosophy, but psychology's contribution has been to bring them within the range of empirical inquiry. They can become real for the student of today. Seldom in human history has a generation of young people been more eager to grapple with the fundamental problems of human existence. The current catchword is *relevance;* students clamor for courses that are relevant. But relevant to what? The challenge to the teacher of psychology is to capitalize on the student concern for relevance, to begin with the problems that for the student are most insistent, to share his concern, and then to lead him toward the recognition of even more fundamental problems. The philosopher's task, presumably, is to help the student to think more clearly. The psychologist can do this too; but his special responsibility is to lead the student to the point at which he will almost automatically say, "Here is a problem for research. We need facts. What facts? How are we to collect them? How are we to test them? How are we to interpret them?" The challenge to the teacher of psychology is to demonstrate that human problems can be solved, or at least clarified, if they are investigated with the attitude and the skills of the scientist.

3. To whom are you teaching psychology?

The first point to make in identifying your students is that you are not teaching psychology just to future teachers of psychology. There will undoubtedly be a good many of these in your classes, but the majority of your students will be young men and women who are not thinking of psychology as a career; whose primary interest is in another subject-matter field; whose professional goals are possibly in law, medicine or industry; or who are taking a course in psychology simply because the subject sounds interesting. You should have something of value to say to all young human beings to whom the world is open, exciting, challenging. The best of your students will honestly want to find out how a psychologist deals scientifically with human problems. Most of them will not be worried about requirements for admission to graduate school. They will put you as a psychologist on the spot, and if you cannot demonstrate the relevance of psychology to the clarification of basic human problems, you will fail as a teacher. With the possible exception of some advanced, preprofessional courses, all undergraduate instruction in psychology should probably be directed toward the nonprofessional student.

4. How are you to teach it?

The methods to be used in the teaching of psychology are in principle no different from the methods required by any other subject.

Many questions of teaching method have been ably discussed in Stanford Ericksen's paper. There is no point in restating his argument. The beginning teacher must, however, be prepared to try out a variety of methods and to select those which he can use most capably in meeting the requirements of the subject and the characteristics of his students. There is no fixed formula. Teaching is an exercise in communication, and successful communication depends on a multitude of factors which the teacher must identify and control. Many of these are rooted in the psychology of motivation, learning, attitude formation, and the like, and every good teacher is, in a practical sense, a good psychologist.

For the teacher of psychology, a few points might be stressed.

a. As a psychologist, he ought to have a special advantage. He is a student of human behavior, and if there are any solid principles in behavioral science he ought to be able to apply them effectively. Teaching is an exercise in applied psychology, and the psychologist who fails does so either because he does not know his subject or because he has not grasped the relation between psychological principles and teaching practices. In both cases he is not only a bad teacher but also a bad psychologist.

b. As a psychologist he is an experimental scientist, and as such he will regard every course he teaches, indeed every lecture, every demonstration, every classroom discussion, and every examination, as an experiment in which he is clearly aware of objectives, hypotheses, controlled and uncontrolled variables, procedures, reliability of observations, and validity of conclusions. This may sound like a cold-blooded approach to teaching, but even a warm-hearted teacher can be intelligently aware of what he is doing.

c. As a scientist he is concerned with evaluation, and as a psychologist he knows a good deal about the methods of evaluating outcomes as related to objectives. The psychologist will be constantly alert to the need for new and better methods of evaluation.

The teacher of psychology is thus presented with a very special challenge, namely, to make his teaching a living demonstration of the practical applicability of his subject. This would seem to suggest that the psychologist ought to be the best teacher on the faculty. He seldom is, for the obvious reason, as the psychologist knows, that skill in teaching requires more than mere mastery of subject matter and technique. The greatest of teachers have skills in communication that they have not acquired through the study of psychology, and the young psychologist might do well to observe such teachers in action.

5. How should you prepare yourself to teach psychology?

The first and obvious answer to a question on preparation is that you must know your subject, but this becomes less obvious as teachers and psychologists ask themselves what their subject really is. If psychology is simply what is presented as psychology in the textbooks and the periodicals, its mastery is a big, but still a finite, task. In some other fields, a simple subject-matter definition may be possible, although it is doubtful. For psychology, however, the subject matter cannot be neatly circumscribed. Psychology's central problem, the understanding of man, leads out into virtually every field of human life. James took it for granted that the psychologist should be well grounded in philosophy, but for him an acquaintance with physiology and neurology was equally important. Today psychologists would have to add such natural-science fields as genetics, ethology, and possibly biochemistry, plus the supporting mathematical skills; and they would also have to add anthropology, sociology, and other social sciences. Back in the late nineteenth century Dilthey argued that the proper approach to the understanding of man is through history, and in recent years the humanistic movement in psychology has come to life again, with its emphasis on literature and the arts as sources of psychological insight. It would seem that to teach psychology properly one would have to have colossal scholarship.

And this is exactly what is suggested here; the psychologist should be the most broadly educated man on the faculty. An ideal that is probably unattainable, but one that defines a direction. If the beginning teacher has had standard graduate training, he will face his first teaching job with confidence in his mastery of a rather narrowly defined subject. He is faced with these two alternatives or with the possibility of several compromises: (1) he may recede into a still more narrowly defined field of specialization and reject everything else as "not in my field" or (2) he may actively broaden his interests, play with new problems, open his mind to the challenges presented to psychology by other disciplines. Of the two, I obviously favor the second; but a compromise ought to be possible.

The compromise I favor is by no means impracticable. The psychologist as a scientist is actively inquiring. As a teacher he is presenting his subject as an on-going operation, and he is inviting his students to share in an adventure of discovery. It would be a sham if he were not himself an active inquirer. This does not necessarily mean that he is constantly grinding out research papers, but it does mean that he is personally involved in the quest for psychological understanding. This may take the form of a research project, but there are many other ways in which the psychologist can be creative— through the projects of his students, through community enterprises, and the like. The important thing is that for him psychology should be not just a subject to be taught but an active inquiry in which his students can become engaged. He will be a poor teacher if he is not himself "engaged"; and he may turn out to be a great teacher if, in spite of stumbling methods, he succeeds in sharing his engagement with his students.

At the same time, the psychologist, as a member of the community, is expected to have wise comments about everything that has to do with human behavior. The standard reaction is to disclaim any competence outside "my own field." This, say some psychologists, is wrong. You, as a psychologist, are fact-minded. You have learned how to take a complex problem and translate it into a set of questions for research. Even if your specialty is color discrimination or proactive inhibition or the functions of the subcortical centers, your skill in the analysis of problems will make a contribution to the community involvement. When the president of the parent-teacher association asks you to assess the effect of violence on television or when your colleague in philosophy asks you about the basis of the esthetic judgment or when the local mayor shares his concern about dissident elements, you will find that, even if you have no ready solutions, your conception of the task of psychology will be broadened. You, as a psychologist, will gain from every association with the larger community. You will gain if you reach out to meet the challenge; you will lose if you retreat into your shell.

THE ANSWERS ARE DIFFICULT

These questions are all easy to ask but quite difficult to answer. I have not tried to conceal my own biases, and it is unlikely anyone will be in complete agreement. It is essential, however, that every beginning teacher answer these and similar questions for himself. Granted that some teachers may be able to perform brilliantly without a plan and without a philosophy, yet the fact remains that most are ordinary persons who need to think things through in advance. Conclusions will vary, but the beginner will be well on the road to becoming a good teacher if (1) he is in love with his subject; (2) he has respect for his students; (3) he is open-minded about method, willing to challenge tradition and to experiment with new procedures; and (4) he regards his subject as a meaningful part of a larger educational enterprise.

Bibliography

James, William. *Principles of Psychology*. 1890.

MacLeod, Robert B. "The Teaching of Psychology and the Psychology We Teach." *American Psychologist* 20 (1965): 344-52.

Wolfle, Dael; Buxton, C. E.; Cofer, C. N.; Gustad, J. W.; MacLeod, R. B.; and McKeachie, W. J. *Improving Undergraduate Instruction in Psychology*. New York: Macmillan Co., 1952.

The Organization
of the Profession

LEWIS MAYHEW

At one time, college teachers served in institutions for which presidents, deans, and board members were clearly responsible. A faculty member could usually settle his own problems and influence major decisions by walking a short distance to the president's office, the door to which was, in theory, always open. That day is gone forever. Public institutions in most states and some private institutions have become parts of statewide systems and agencies in which power to make decisions is far from where professors can influence decisions through direct intervention.

PROBLEMS AND ISSUES

Today the college teacher serves in a complex system under complex conditions of on- and off-campus pressures, tensions, obligations, and —paradoxically—both expanded power and restricted freedom. Such conditions have created issues and problems that affect his teaching and his functioning in general.

The young professor should understand the reasons for the changed conditions, the issues created and their implications for him, the system of which he is a part, the sources of information and help available to him, and the opportunities he has to influence higher education. He should begin, however, by selecting the kind of institution in which he wishes to serve, deciding how best to know and use its mechanisms and resources, and at least recognizing an academic macrocosm.

Enrollment growth. Many of the changes and the issues have resulted from the increased enrollment of students and the rapid growth of institutions, both of which have been caused in part by the increased affluence of the nation. In a period of rapid growth, many institutions are forced to change their principal functions—for instance, teachers' colleges become comprehensive universities; urban universities, set up to serve a local community, must serve an entire state.

As institutions change their functions, they expect professors to perform different activities, and thus they provoke a number of ten-

---

Dr. Mayhew is professor of education, Stanford University, and past-president, American Association for Higher Education.

sions. For example, a professor who likes to teach and was rewarded for doing so in a teachers' college finds after transferring to a university that he is expected to do research and to publish, for neither of which he has skill or interest. If he is nonetheless rewarded, those who do research and were recruited for that purpose are resentful. If he is not rewarded, he naturally feels penalized.

As institutions have increased in size and taken on new functions, the academic profession has gained new power and prominence, to both the advantage and disadvantage of college teachers. They are, for instance, subjected to great temptations by demands made on their time. When government, corporations, and other institutions offer opportunities for well-compensated consulting work or contract research and when the professor's own institution emphasizes the value of high national visibility for its faculty members, professors are sorely tempted to spend more time off than on campus. They are gratified not only by the financial rewards but also by the satisfaction the ego finds in being in demand. But the cost to the professors and to their institutions is high, for the energies that are consumed off campus are not available to students or for institutional responsibilities. It would seem that this problem could be solved by limiting such work to a day a week, but such a solution would not work. The market for academic talent is increasing, and the more professors and institutions respond to the market, the greater the demand for their services.

Military-industrial ties. A closely related issue and one with ethical and professional implications for college teachers is the association of institutions of higher education with the military-industrial complex. Some institutions have begun to function more for the welfare of the military and individual corporations than for that of society at large. Some universities have made their services available to corporations and the military, have spawned new corporations, have given board memberships to industrial leaders who, in turn, have facilitated mutually beneficial arrangements for the university and corporation, and have even allied themselves with powerful political elements for the benefit of one segment of society. Universities have profited from such arrangements. Endowments have increased through wise holding of growth stocks. Military-supported research has helped professors with their work, and the proximity of universities to research-based industries has contributed to the welfare of both. But the costs have been high to both professors and institutions. Some contract research has raised an ethical question about war policy. Some contract research has diverted institutional effort from the directions in which it would normally move. And some institutional decisions have been vulnerable to the suspicion that they were made for other than educational purposes. Eventually each faculty member must inform himself of the implications of such arrangements for himself and must help chart a reasonable course for his institution.

Together these two issues present the university professor with an intense value-conflict. He is attracted by the virtues and rewards of research, scholarship, and publication. Moreover, a teacher often sees his future as closely bound to the recognition he receives from his off-campus colleagues in his discipline as to the institution he serves. At the same time he feels bound by the tradition of a professor as a teacher of the young, a tradition recently reinforced by the students' strident demands that they be heard and served. Like teachers generally, he wants to serve students and to earn their respect and love, but he clearly sees the dangers of doing so, especially in large prestige universities. Promotions just do not go rapidly to those whose reputations are based chiefly on teaching and advising students.

Student demands. In the meantime, the professor's conflict is intensified by students' demands for power and influence. Although no one knows the extent to which students' demands for power and influence will go, or for how long, their demands must be considered as a significant issue. Some students, concerned about such social malfunctioning as the failure to insure the civil rights of minority groups, to reduce poverty, and to end a seemingly unjust war, are disrupting routine on some campuses. There has apparently evolved a loose confederation of radical student-groups with central headquarters and considerable communication and cooperation between campuses. The techniques of protest found useful at one place are being exported to another. Some persons have argued that there is a nationwide student-conspiracy to bring all of higher education to a stop so that it can be rebuilt closer to the students' own ideals. Faculty members must decide how to respond to militancy. Some appear to have joined in support of what they believe are legitimate demands, while others are cooperating apparently in hopes of using the force generated to press demands of their own. And still others, possibly a majority, see that the efforts of militant students will serve only to attract a backlash against them and all of higher education from the larger society, especially from the political segments. It seems clear that if destructive student-protests continue, legislatures will be tempted to reduce support and even pass highly restrictive legislation, which may then lead to an even more militant stand by students.

Academic freedom. Professors face a different order of issues in what they see as threats to academic freedom. At one time threats to the freedom of professors seemed to come chiefly from administrators who did not want institutional tranquility disturbed. That time too is long past, but new and more serious threats are coming from off-campus groups and agencies. As the cost of higher education has increased, especially the share provided from taxes, political agencies have felt constrained to scrutinize collegiate operations more closely and to proscribe behavior believed to be not in the public interest. Although teachers may conform generally to public expectations, proscribed behavior makes them feel as though their principles were being sacrificed. They can, however, advance principles so far that they bring about a confrontation with off-campus power. Illustrative is the decision of several faculty members at the University of California to employ, as a guest lecturer in a credit course, a Negro militant who was under judicial review. This sparked a reaction from the governor and legislative leaders and a decision by the board of regents to deny faculty the right to expose youths to a convicted rapist. So the issue was joined, and no easy resolution is possible. Increasingly there will be episodes which professors will regard as legislative or political outrages but which the public will regard as justifiable.

Institutional governance. At the same time the behavior of some professors is being controlled by off-campus agencies, professors are seeking a greater voice in institutional governance, even to the point of hegemony. They are even responding to the possibility of potential control. Faculty members want not only to decide who their colleagues shall be, what subjects are to be taught, and which students are to be accepted but also to have a say in who their leaders shall be and how institutional resources shall be expended.

Faculty members believe that the curriculum or subjects to be taught should be their responsibility. Yet pressures from off campus have begun to limit their exercise of such a power. Senior institutions sometimes directly control curricular content in junior colleges. Statewide coordinating councils attempt to decide which institutions will teach which courses. Accrediting agencies attempt to insure that each institution offers those courses believed by the agency to be essential. And, of course, the real or imagined requirements of graduate schools determine what four-year, bachelor's degree-granting institutions offer. These off-campus forces clearly believe that the faculty of an institution or department will not be responsive to the needs of the larger society if it is not controlled, while faculty members see such control as an intrusion on their proper rights and responsibilities.

To the extent that faculties succeed in gaining hegemony, to that extent they become professionalized, self-serving examples of syndicalism less and less responsive to the demands of the society they were appointed to serve. The slowness with which British universities have responded to the increasing educational needs and desires of the mass of the British people is in part attributable to the syndicalism of British faculties. Present demands for well-trained faculty members are so great that faculties can insist on almost complete power. But the more power they gain, the greater the possibilities of a significant revulsion in public feeling toward higher education. Indeed, in 1968 thoughtful men could maintain that if faculties persisted in seeking hegemony, no capable person would consider becoming a college president (there were 400 vacancies that year) and eventually the public would revoke not only the new but also the traditional rights of faculty members, such as tenure and academic freedom.

But college teachers have ways of protecting not only their traditional rights but also themselves against backlash, retribution, or intrusion on their prerogatives. To protect themselves from specialized accrediting agencies, they created the National Commission on Accrediting to monitor those who would monitor others. Through trade unionism, they can exert power against the institutions and the state systems.

At one time professors generally felt that their professional image would not allow them to use union techniques of collective bargaining, economic sanctions, and strikes. But, beginning in junior colleges and then spreading to state colleges and universities, a trade union point of view has become more and more acceptable. Even the American Association of University Professors could reason that in some circumstances a strike of professors would not be against the public interest. Now, trade unionism is not necessarily bad. Some administrators have suggested that it would be easier to arrive at work contracts every three or four years through collective bargaining with a union than to arrive at decisions by consensus as each issue arises. Others believe that governance through cooperation, shared responsibility, or a corporate faculty is still best for a university. In 1968 there was no clear evidence on whether an adversary or a cooperative system of governance would eventually prevail in American higher education. The one clear fact was that each faculty member would be forced to face the issue and to search for ways of resolving it.

Student rights. At one time a professor's freedom to deal with students was virtually untouched by the courts. Institutions and their faculties were judged to serve in loco parentis and were accorded all of the powers which parents have. They could accept or expel students and were not obliged to give reasons. They could organize courses and require students to take them without allowing students any recourse if they believed that the courses failed to benefit them. Institutions and their faculties still have much of this power, but the courts are becoming interested in relations between students and professors. As citizens, students are guaranteed procedural rights, and institutions are expected to use procedures approximating those used in civil and criminal litigation in controversy over academic matters. While the courts have not influenced the teacher to the extent that other agencies and forces have, the direction is toward more carefully defined relationships.

An unsystematic system. One other matter should be mentioned before ending this discussion of issues and problems: the way in which broad educational policy is set in the United States. While the influence of the federal government is strong, no central ministry of education determines policy. That is still established through the interaction of many frequently conflicting and contending groups. Through interlocking systems of committees, commissions, and organizations, higher education expresses its needs and desires. An individual professor who wishes to understand the system thus must learn to operate in this unsystematic system.

COPING WITH THE CONFLICTS

Although these problems and issues affecting the professional life of the teacher are as yet unsolved or unresolved, there are policies, organizations, and sources of information that can help him understand the issues and cope with the problems.

State and regional systems. Of all the new influences on the changing role of professors, none is more potent than the new regional and state systems of higher education. In 1957, ten states had developed suprainstitutional coordinating boards or councils with general powers to do long-range planning for public higher education, to collect data, and to recommend the locations of new programs. By 1967, only ten states did not have such agencies, and while the specific powers assigned vary from state to state, they generally are those just mentioned plus the powers to review institutional budgets, to select sites for new campuses, and to approve or disapprove new programs. In one state this last power extends to approval of individual courses.

A first order of business for the coordinating body is to create a state master-plan for higher education, which typically seeks to identify several types of institutions, each limited to a specific purpose. State admissions policies are designed to direct students into appropriate types of institutions. For example, in California the state university is expected to concentrate on graduate and professional education, the state colleges on upper division and graduate work to the master's level, and the junior colleges on lower-division work. In Florida there are the state universities, each with an assigned role and scope, and the junior colleges. The importance of the state coordinating agencies to an individual professor can be great; they determine such matters as whether faculty members will be encouraged to do research, whether new programs responsive to local needs can be funded, how large an institution will be allowed to grow, and what powers the administration of a single campus will be allowed to use.

State coordinating bodies were created in part because of the earlier successful experiences some states had had with regional compacts. The first of these was the Southern Regional Education Board, which has attempted to help southern states meet manpower needs through cooperative development of high-cost programs such as medical training. The New England and Western states have since banded together to form similar enterprises. These boards publish reports, conduct programs for the improvement of various kinds of collegiate education, and assist the states in cooperatively conducting activities beyond the resources of any one state. Private institutions have begun to cooperate in order to enrich programs and to share the expense of particularly high-cost activities. The Great Lakes College Association and the Associated Colleges of the Midwest represent one kind of consortium, the twenty-one state associations of private colleges another kind. But they all seek to help institutions plan so that there may be no unnecessary duplication of effort to drain an institution's resources.

National organizations. State and regional compacts and coordinating bodies provide a semiformal structure for higher education, and in their day to day decisions they are making higher education policy. But a less formal system also does similar work. The network of organizations and associations, many with headquarters in Washington, D. C., provides information, makes policy statements, and seeks to influence legislation on higher education. There are several types of these, each serving a specific clientele.

Several organizations represent specific sorts of institutions, such as junior colleges or prestige graduate institutions. These, as well as the institutions they represent, are affiliated with the American Council on Education. Through publications, conferences, policy statements, and legislative influence, the council seeks to represent higher education as reflected in the needs of institutions.

Of generally less political significance, although of considerable professional significance to individual professors, are the learned societies representing the various subjects or disciplines. It is through the channels of these societies that the marketplace for college teachers frequently operates—or seems to operate. The American Council of Learned Societies is the logical focus for these professional organizations, although it is of limited policy-force.

A third sort of organization seeks to represent individuals active in higher education. The American Association for Higher Education, the various organizations of people active in student personnel work, the Association for Institutional Research, and the American Association of University Professors are illustrative. While there is, at present, no coordinating body for this sort of organization, the officers and professional staffs do work closely together and consult on positions regarding legislation and national educational policy. Through overlapping memberships, interlocking committees, ad hoc committees, and commissions, these associations insure that the national higher-education system is responsive to national needs, even though it lacks a formal structure.

Research and information. No reasonable decisions can be made about higher education practice or policy without some reasonably reliable information. Until recently such information was not generally available, and more is still needed. However, this condition is rapidly changing. Institutions have created offices of institutional research, which have generated a great deal of information. Largely as a result of efforts of such organizations as the College Entrance Examination Board, the Educational Testing Service, and the American College Testing Program, the information is reported in comparable terms. Several universities have created centers for the study of higher education, which conduct research about types of institutions, flow of students, cost of higher education, and the like. Columbia, for example, has created the Institute for Higher Education, which has produced a series of almost forty reports of considerable value to individual professors.

In addition to the information mentioned, there is the work of some 400 professors of higher education and their graduate students. Since 1955, when higher education was recognized as a field of study, the professors and their students have produced a substantial volume of histories, evaluation studies, case studies, and monographs about higher education. Although much of what is published is superficial or of limited interest, as the volume increases (as it has each year since 1955), the number of significant works increases at a still more rapid rate. Higher education, however, has not yet developed effective bibliographic or abstracting services that can quickly reveal what is known. The American Association for Higher Education does produce an essay on the literature of higher education and a digest of what the periodical press says about the subject; the *Chronicle of Higher Education,* a weekly newspaper, lists new books; and several universities have created computer systems for collecting information. But the distribution of information about higher education in general is still quite primitive as compared with that in such fields as chemistry and psychology.

Much more readily available to individual professors is information about salaries, fringe benefits, and—strangely enough—the quality of institutions. The American Association of University Professors has in recent years collected and published information on salaries paid at most institutions, grading them on an *AA* to *F* scale. Every other year the National Education Association publishes a report on salaries and compensation, which lists salaries paid by type of institution and by region. The Association of American Colleges has sponsored and published studies of faculty benefits and a study of compensation for administrators. While these will become dated rather quickly, they do serve as important benchmarks and will, beyond doubt, be redone from time to time. The American Council on Education has produced a study of the quality of graduate education, which ranks graduate schools by their reputations. The College Entrance Examination Board publishes its Freshman Class Profiles, which reveal the ability of students attending a number of different institutions, and several individual authors have published guides to colleges and universities, which attempt some ranking of them. A notable example is the *Comparative Guide to American Colleges* by James Cass and Max Birnbaum. The U. S. Office of Education publishes annually *The Education Directory: Part III, Higher Education*, which lists accredited institutions and institutions whose credits are accepted on transfer; the American Council on Education publishes a directory of four-year colleges and universities and one of junior colleges.

Ethics and guidelines. Although the college-teaching profession does not generally accept a code of ethics, as does the medical or legal profession, there are several documents that are ethical in character and that help guide some institutional and professorial conduct. Several of the national professional organizations have prepared the Joint Statement on Rights and Freedoms of Students, published in the winter 1967 *AAUP Bulletin.* It urges open access to higher education, proclaims the personal worth and dignity of students, argues for the confidentiality of student records, demands freedom of association and a freedom of inquiry and expression, and stresses the need for procedural rights of students involved in disciplinary problems. The American Association of University Professors, through a series of policy statements and letters of advice, has demanded the freedom of the scholar to study and teach as he wishes, insisted that tenure contracts be respected, urged that faculty members be accorded rights to determine academic policy, and served, in general, as guardian of the profession.[1] However, none of these statements gives particular guidance to professors for dealing with the newer features in American higher education, and none offers counsel on a situation in which a decision of a state system is contrary to local campus desires. For example, if a local campus decides to appoint a professor but the systemwide head terminates the appointment, what stance should be taken, and how? There is no statement on teachers' relationships with

1. Louis Joughin, ed., *Academic Freedom and Tenure.*

a nationwide confederation of radical students such as Students for a Democratic Society. Nor are there statements binding on professors or institutions regarding political action or attempts to influence state and federal legislation. Some persons argue that professors and institutions should take a stand not only on legislation directly relevant to higher education but on other matters of foreign and domestic policy; others argue that any stand would jeopardize academic freedom. Eventually guidelines must be developed, but for the moment a professor is expected to exercise his own judgment in the light of his own conscience.

RELATING TO THE COMPLEX

What has been described thus far are some critical issues affecting professors, some of the dominant characteristics of a national system of higher education that have contributed either to the development of issues or to their resolution, and some sources of information. Now it becomes necessary to ask and answer the question whether the individual professor can or should relate to this complex system. This question leaves the professor in a quandary about whether an individual can in any way affect these vast, seemingly impersonal forces and systems.

First, it should be observed that a few persons, through their own efforts and through their understanding of campus conditions, seem to have made a considerable difference. A few years ago Jerold Zacharias was able to galvanize professors of physics into undertaking a revision of high school physics courses that resulted in major changes in college physics. Arthur Bestor and a few others did call public attention to the training of public school teachers; their efforts, reinforced by the opinion of such men as James B. Conant, did force schools of education to reexamine and to modify their practices. And organizations, through the thoughts and efforts of their members, have from time to time profoundly affected higher-education policy. The American Association of University Professors, through its salary ranking, has helped improve the economic condition of the profession; and the American Association of Higher Education, through the efforts of its executive secretary, helped establish the federal college housing loan program and helped maintain the loan features of the National Defense Education Act. Individuals are not without influence.

Individual professors may even be classified by their use of influence, but it is most relevant here to classify them as locals or nationals. *Locals* are those who gain greatest satisfaction from teaching, serving on institutional committees, and generally being highly regarded on their home campuses. *Nationals,* on the other hand, seek to identify with national groups, involve themselves deeply in off-campus con-

sultation and research, and gain their satisfaction from a national reputation. Now, both of these groups are valuable. The national systems
could not operate without professors who were willing to ride the air
lines and be away from home much of the time. And, of course, a
single institution would quickly fail were it not for local professors
who "tend store." But each group pays a price. A national may very
likely be without high honor on his own campus and may indeed be
quite lonely when not on trips. And the local may not receive the
advances in rank and salary that he deserves, because he has not
established a national reputation. Quite clearly, national professors
have the best opportunity to affect broad policy, but local professors
can also be influential if they are willing to use some of the tools or
techniques available to them.

Speaking and publishing. Increasingly there are conferences, for-
ums, and publications that allow professors (nationals and locals) to
speak out about the problems of higher education and occasionally to
be heard. The National Conference on Higher Education, held each
March in Chicago, and its sixty-odd section meetings provide a forum
on which professors can express and debate their ideas.

The publication of conference proceedings has become a rather large
business; perhaps a third of all books about higher education published
in a given year are of this sort. Although much of this material probably goes unread, there is always the chance that a conference paper
will become influential. William Arrowsmith, a professor of classics at
the University of Texas, at an annual meeting of the American Council on Education, helped focus attention on the poor preparation for
teaching that typical graduate programs provide. Professional journals such as the *Journal for Higher Education, Liberal Education,* or
the *Educational Record* provide outlets for articles. Their editors are
constantly searching for thoughtful writing that can contribute to
national thinking about higher education. Specific mention should
be made of the *Chronicle of Higher Education,* which digests the
content of books and reports in the form of news stories, and a new
journal *Change,* which will allow individuals to describe innovations
that may ultimately change the course of higher education.

Committee work. Much stress has been placed on the informal network of committees, commissions, and advisory boards. It is through
these agencies that individuals can perhaps be most influential, especially if they serve on several at the same time. Influence is accretive,
and the person who in one year serves as president of the American
Association for Higher Education, as a member of the advisory committees of the Educational Records Bureau and the Educational
Testing Service, as consultant to the American Council on Education
and the College Entrance Examination Board, and as a member of a

steering committee for several national research projects has an opportunity to present ideas to several different groups and to use the complex knowledge he gains in those groups to reinforce ideas he supports. But how does an individual come to be invited to serve in such capacities? There is no clear answer, but organizations are constantly searching for people willing to work and to contribute wisdom. Just as effective committee work on a campus leads to increased influence, so effective committee work in national groups leads to more opportunities.

Although state systems cause problems, they too serve as a device by which the individual professor can influence higher education. Systems typically conduct much business through intercollege committees, which consider faculty salaries, articulation, graduate study, and institutional role and scope. While these committees are generally advisory to the legitimate authority of a board, they nonetheless have the authority that comes from expertise. Boards thus are open to recommendations on professional matters when made by responsible committees composed of faculty members. Somehow the experience of dealing with such a problem as articulation of junior and senior colleges for an entire state helps faculty members to broaden their own perspectives and to think in educational, rather than disciplinary, terms.

Gaining a wider view. Essential for committee activities is a broad view of the fabric of higher education, a view which does not come naturally to graduate students or professors immersed in the details of a single field of study. But young professors are being offered increasing opportunities to take time off and gain different perspectives. Several of the regional accrediting agencies have created internships in order to develop broad-visioned people who can serve as consultants or examiners for many different institutions. The Phillips Foundation and the American Council on Education have conducted internship programs designed to convert faculty members into administrators. Each summer the Danforth Foundation conducts a three-week workshop for four faculty members from each of twenty-five institutions. During this period professors have a chance to hear, read, and think about the transcendent issues of higher education with apparently considerable value to themselves and their careers. For more than twenty years the North Central Association Study of Liberal Arts Education has also conducted workshops, which have given well over a thousand different professors time and stimulation to think about higher education in its broad sense.

The bargaining position. Professors may, and do, gain influence through more direct and personal ways. The academic market is not a completely free market, but it is nontheless free enough to allow individual professors to bargain with institutions for their services, and in the aggregate this bargaining sets the tone for all of higher education. From 1955 on, well-qualified faculty members have been in short supply, and institutions have reduced teaching loads, increased salaries and fringe benefits, and made greater provisions for research in order to attract and hold professors. While market conditions may change and faculty bargaining may be reduced, this is not likely to happen for at least several more years. Thus, what someone has called academic poker is likely to go on. In academic poker the college instructor obtains an offer from another institution and then uses it as a bargaining element to improve his local situation. The player must realize, of course, that there is a limit to the number of bluffs he can run, but he probably can manage one or two. So widespread has been the development of bargaining that faculty stability on many campuses has been shaken as instructors take posts knowing that if they do not like things, they can and will move elsewhere. Individual efforts have made the American college teacher a member of a truly mobile profession.

The collective version of this bargaining, of course, is reflected in various kinds of adversary relationships between faculty and administration. Several states have provided for collective bargaining by either faculty senates or a union, and such bargaining seems likely to cover most interests in higher education, from salaries to selection of administrators. In states having complex systems, such as New York, a statewide faculty senate or a state-based union can thus allow faculty members to develop great power and to influence state policy. This is not to suggest that collective bargaining is either a good or a bad thing. As indicated earlier, there is a belief that shared responsibility and cooperative governance have much to commend them. But adversary bargaining is a recognized form and is available if faculty members wish to use it. Apparently it does not deny professional ethics or image as was originally believed.

This section has sought to establish the fact that individual professors must interact with an increasingly complicated system of higher education. Consider the professor of biology who teaches principles validated by a National Science Foundation grant in a classroom built in part by funds supplied by the National Institutes of Health. His course was approved by a statewide coordinating council and is offered to students supported by a National Defense Education Act loan. These students live in residence halls built with a college housing loan allocated to the institution by a state committee designated by the governor but whose members were recommended by a citizens committee for higher education. The professor's tenure appointment is protected by legislation suggested by the American Association of

University Professors, and his rights to decide on the tenure appointment of other professors are contained in a constitution suggested by the American Association for Higher Education. His students will be admitted to college on the basis of tests prepared by a large independent test bureau, their eligibility for scholarship funds established by a different organization. He has more Negro students than ever before because of pressure brought to bear by a Black Student Union, which is loosely related to the national Students for a Democratic Society. Next week the professor must vote on whether he wishes a statewide senate or the American Federation of Teachers to represent him in collective bargaining. His own salary is tied to a decision his institution must make on a new medical school recommended by a regional compact and supported by his state coordinating council for higher education. On all of these, as well as many other matters, the professor can affect the outcome. The question is, will he?

Bibliography

Bowles, Frank H. *The Refounding of the College Board, 1948–1963.* New York: College Entrance Examination Board, 1967.
Reveals the emergence of major powers in the establishment of higher educational policy; includes a complicated array of paraeducational agencies and organizations. It also reveals the considerable prophetic powers of the author.

Brown, David G. *The Mobile Professors.* Washington: American Council on Education, 1967.
Describes the characteristics of the marketplace for college teachers and how both individuals and institutions seek to use the marketplace. Concludes that the academic marketplace is far from a free market.

Brubacher, John S. *Bases for Policy in Higher Education.* New York: McGraw-Hill Book Co., 1965.
Attempts to show how higher-education policy has historically been established and discusses some policy issues that must be resolved in the near future.

Caplow, Theodore, and McGee, Reece J. *The Academic Marketplace.* New York: Doubleday & Co., 1965.
Contains valuable descriptions of how individuals obtain positions, move, and establish their reputations.

Cass, James, and Birnbaum, Max. *Comparative Guide to American Colleges.* New York: Harper & Row, Publishers, 1968.
Lists all accredited four-year colleges alphabetically and comments on campus life, academic environment, and kinds of students attracted.

Chambers, M. M. *The Colleges and the Courts, 1962–1966.* Danville, Ill.: Interstate Printers & Publishers, 1967.
One of a series of books summarizing and commenting on court decisions impinging on higher education.

Coons, Arthur G. *Crises in California Higher Education.* Los Angeles: Ward Ritchie Press, 1968.
Describes in detail the development of the California master plan for higher education and the evolution of the coordinating council as a supra-institutional agency; reveals in a case study the growing impingement of off-campus forces on individual faculty members.

Cowles Guide to Graduate Schools. New York: Cowles Education Corp., 1968.
Presents alphabetic listing of institutions offering graduate work and the subjects and degrees offered.

Efficiency of Freedom, The. Baltimore: Johns Hopkins Press, 1959.
Reports on the various intrusions of state government into the control of institutions and suggests guidelines and criteria by which the public interests can be served and institutional freedoms preserved.

Greenberg, Daniel S. *The Politics of Pure Science.* New York: New American Library, 1967.
Shows how federal involvement in university scientific research came about during World War II and how present scientific-research policy is established.

Ingraham, Mark H. *The Outer Fringe.* Madison: University of Wisconsin Press, 1965.
Summarizes the frequency and type of fringe benefits available to faculty in American colleges and universities.

Ingraham, Mark H., and King, Francis P. *The Mirror of Brass.* Madison: University of Wisconsin Press, 1968.
Presents norms of salaries and perquisites provided for first-, second-, and third-echelon collegiate administrators.

Joughin, Louis, ed. *Academic Freedom and Tenure: A Handbook of the American Association of University Professors.* Madison: University of Wisconsin Press, 1967.
Presents basic documents and a number of letters and memoranda elucidating emerging ethical principles and principles regarding the reduction of controversy.

Minter, John W. *The Individual and the System.* Boulder, Colo.: Western Interstate Commission for Higher Education, 1967.
Contains papers on recent student protests against the impersonality of higher education and a number of suggestions by which individuals and institutions can be responsive to student demands and desires.

Ridgeway, James. *The Closed Corporation: American Universities in Crisis.* New York: Random House, 1968.
Attempts to show the rapprochement between big business, big military, big government, and big universities and how these are developing policies at times antithetical to the needs of the larger society. It probably is slightly overdrawn but close enough to reality to support the subtitle.

Singletary, Otis A., and Newman, Jane P., eds. *American Universities and Colleges.* 10th ed. Washington: American Council on Education, 1968.
Contains detailed information on four-year institutions of higher education, covering student characteristics, administrative structure, and programs and degrees offered.

Finding the Levers

The Folkways and Mores of Campus Governance

HAROLD HODGKINSON

Young faculty members, or those preparing for the academic life, must face the fact that the first year or two in the first teaching position is often fraught with doubts, tensions, and insecurities. These are sometimes accidental, sometimes intentional initiations into the rite-of-passage system. A large number of young faculty find themselves in positions that are not quite as advertised, and if it were not for the enormous mobility of faculty from campus to campus, many more would leave the teaching profession.

Much of the young faculty's difficulty comes from a sense of ignorance and powerlessness, of not knowing how the campus in which they find themselves really works, of having no good sources of information and little power or influence in the academic and administrative arenas. Although the new faculty member has graduated from the role of student, he finds that once again he is playing the subordinate role to his "peers," who will judge, along with the administration, his fitness for tenure and promotion. As a newly minted professional, he often finds that he teaches the courses that no one else wants to teach, has difficulty in getting on important committees but is automatically selected for participation on the Joint Faculty-Student Committee to Consider the Renaming of the Gymnasium, acts as advisor to freshmen but not often to senior and graduate students, and does not go to lunch with the dean or department chairman. He is told that promotion and tenure will depend on his teaching, but of course research must not be forgotten. He is to be popular with his students, but not too popular, especially with the best students.

It is not that people give him devious answers, but that they give him contradictory ones, as complex institutions are almost always internally inconsistent. In that he is near the bottom of the academic hierarchy, he will get more inconsistent answers than those faculty members who have been there longer. People will inform him of procedures to be followed, but the information will be in mimeographed

Dr. Hodgkinson is project director, Center for Research and Development in Higher Education, University of California, Berkeley. This paper is in part a product of the American Association for Higher Education Campus Governance Project of which he is associate director.

form, as it is for new students. He will not know whom to see to get things done, and, more important, he will not know whom not to see. (Avoiding the ineffectual person in the hierarchy is one mark of the seasoned professional.)

This short paper attempts to present some of the things to look for and watch out for, so that meaningful participation in campus governance might come earlier for the new academic and he might come to feel that the campus is a piece of wondrous machinery that works *for* him rather than *on* him.

Although many experienced college and university faculty take the position that getting involved in campus politics will leave no time for teaching and research, it is nevertheless true that even teaching and research activities require a campus structure for acquiring the things that are necessary. Those who remove themselves from the battlefield entirely should therefore feel little remorse if the system does not meet their needs. On the other hand, it is true that educational politics is the major specialization of some faculty members who get little accomplished in any other area. For some a committee meeting has all the fascination of a gaming table at Reno—they become addicted to the roll of the dice and the changes in fortune as the game proceeds. Governance has ceased being a means and has become an end in itself. Outside these extremes of zero and absolute involvement, a person needs some criteria, some "institutional superego" or gyroscope that will allow him to be selective in the areas in which he will take part. One of the best of these criteria is that of enlightened self-interest. If the task offered is one in which the person thinks he can be productive and in which he will learn from participation, then he probably ought to get involved. But how can one decide in advance whether or not participation on a given committee or activity will be meaningful? Information about how the campus works is necessary for this decision, and here are some ways such information can be acquired.

THE WORKING HISTORY

One thing that new faculty can put to good use is a short history of the institution, one based not on the catalog description but on who was actually responsible for the program as it exists. Who are the people who have effected changes, and who are those who have the power to impede change? The "working history" can usually be put together quite accurately by keeping one's ears open at social affairs and at the lunch table. Often, department and committee sessions will provide the major shape of the working history. The new teacher will also find that he spends more time with students than with his colleagues, and students can be a very good source for the working history, although their interpretation of who accomplished what and who the "good guys" were (or are) may be at variance with the interpretations of faculty and administration. The new faculty member needs to see the institution as the sum total of the efforts of others, some of whom have left or died, some of whom are very much still on the scene. With a good working history even a first-year teacher can begin to estimate how people and groups will respond to situations and *why* they do so.

TYPES OF CAMPUSES

One problem of the new faculty member is that he tends to compare the first campus where he teaches with the institution in which he did graduate work (often the only campus he remembers well). This often means that he misses the teaching potential of his location. Every campus presents a slightly different set of assets and liabilities for the new teacher—the trick is to find out what they are as soon as possible. One way to look at campus types is to consider what students who come to the institution think they "need," compared to what the institution wants to do to them ("press"). Some of the major variations are listed below in abbreviated form.

Vocational. The students come primarily because they wish to be certified for a job that is important to them. Studying is a means toward this end. The faculty see their major job as certifying that graduates are fit to enter these vocations.

Collegiate. The students come largely to make social contacts that will be useful to them in later life and to have a good time. Fraternities, sororities, and active social programs typify these campuses. The faculty are fairly relaxed in their maintenance of standards. Alumni groups have considerable influence.

Intellectual. Students here tend to be interested in learning either for its own sake or in order to become a permanent member of the academic community. Their approach to intellect is a highly structured one. The structure is imposed largely by the faculty, who provide very heavy reading assignments and frequent tests. (Indeed, faculty are often judged by the length of their reading lists.)

Expressive. Almost a derivative of the intellectual campus, the expressive also stresses the intellect, but as a vehicle for personal expression and communication. Intellect here begins with the personality and works out, whereas on intellectual campuses the student prostrates himself before the discipline. The creative arts are usually strong at expressive institutions; science teaching is excellent at intellectual ones. On expressive campuses the faculty tend to see their task as a Socratic one, to elicit the best the student has to offer. The faculty often play a counseling role in their teaching.

Protective. A number of American colleges see their chief role as that of an umbrella, protecting the innocent student from the harsh rains of society. Social life is heavily regulated, and the living environment is considered an important part of what the college teaches. Adults on these campuses often become what Waller calls "Museums of Virtue"—exhibiting values and behavior no longer commonly practiced but to which they feel college students should be exposed. Students often come seeking certainty and closure on questions of philosophy and values, while students at expressive institutions seem to enjoy playing with ambiguity and paradox.

These five types of campus culture are of course not pure—any campus will show elements of all five. But if one looks carefully, there will probably be evidence of a central tendency or major push in one or two of these five directions. There are obvious conflicts in a new teacher who shares expressive values and finds himself on a protective campus, and such a teacher might be well advised to keep his commitments about teaching to himself until he has scouted the ground. If his teaching style comes quickly to attract the potential activist students, he may be branded with a reputation that will be difficult to live with. (On many campuses, new faculty are classified rather quickly by colleagues and administration, and these first impressions are hard to alter.) There are also departmental variations along these cultural lines—often one will find a very intellectual psychology or history department next to a very expressive humanities or literature department. Moreover, within departments there are often factions which resemble the five cultures, along with pure and applied distinctions and micro and macro orientations. Often the new faculty member unthinkingly commits himself to one of these factions by an off-hand remark and later finds that his place in the department is already decided.

TALL OR FLAT ORGANIZATION

At the "tall" end of the scale one finds the institution that, in terms of power and accountability, operates as a pyramid with the president and board at the top controlling everything. Little authority is delegated to other groups, communication is carefully controlled at levels of the hierarchy, and people tend to operate according to explicit patterns ("by the book"). At the "flat" end of the scale one finds groups of faculty and students as the core units of organization, usually in a departmental form, with the administration operating as a link between them. There are few administrative levels of status, and groupings of persons shift quite easily as their concerns change. Behavior tends to be worked out on the spot instead of being looked up in the manual. Clearly almost all colleges and universities fall between these extremes, but one question should be worth mentioning: Who *really* makes decisions here? Are faculty actions definite, or are they recommendations to the administration? Who speaks for the faculty, the whole body or a representative assembly such as a senate or an executive committee? To whom do they speak? Are departmental chairmen elected by colleagues or appointed by administration? How is a new president selected? Who chairs faculty meetings, and why? How is the membership of major faculty and all-campus committees established? Is the dean the faculty's man or the president's man, or both? One good way to ascertain the answers to these questions is to isolate a common activity and follow its development—for example, follow all the steps necessary for a new course to become part of a department's instructional program.

COMMUNICATION SYSTEMS

On every campus there is a formal system of communication. It is visible in the line-staff organization chart, or it can be derived in descending order from the officials listed in the catalog. There is another system that may be more important. It is usually more horizontal, more direct, more functional than the formal one. It may involve secretaries, assistants to major officers, clerks, buildings and grounds staff, nurses, food-service workers, and many others who have no place in the formal communication structure. Yet these are often the people who must be seen to get things done or to get accurate information. The complexity of this system may vary with institutional size; on small campuses the network usually covers all departments, while on large campuses it may center in the department or the administrative subunits. It generally runs on necessity, not form; information that must be transmitted will be transmitted in this way even though there is no formal channel. Department secretaries are almost always involved, as are the secretaries and assistants to the major administrators. The system works in much the same way as the system of sidewalks on the campus—the concrete sections are like the formal structure, the downtrodden grass where people make their own pathways is like the informal one.

If the eyes and ears are kept open, it is quite easy to locate the important people in this system. One advantage of this approach is that the information is easier to evaluate—it tends to be either obvious gossip or obviously accurate. For example, if a new teacher really wanted to find out how he would be promoted and evaluated, and on what grounds, he might find that some faculty colleagues support the rhetoric in the faculty handbook and that the registrar, senior students, or perhaps a long-term secretary is a better source. (Certainly the registrar's office would be a good source of information on grading practices, for example—the young faculty member whose grades are too high will often find this fact held against him. The registrar often knows whether the department marks on the curve and whether this particular department assesses teaching quality by grading, student reactions, or some other means.) In many institutions the rating of teaching effectiveness is done almost purely on word-of-mouth reputation and social contacts. In fact, there are occasional references to situations in which a young faculty member was given tenure because of the social acceptability of his wife, and some in which tenure was denied because of her lack of social acceptability. These, however, are extremely rare. For some reasons yet unfathomed, it is not easy for the new teacher to get good information on what is expected of him. He is to be a good teacher, yes, but what is considered to be good teaching? Often one can unobtrusively pick up this information through the informal communication system when consulting one's senior colleagues in the department might be interpreted as being overly "pushy." The distinction between junior- and senior-faculty membership is often more important than one would expect, and like any initiation rite, the element of mystery is present from the initiate's point of view. But he obviously should have these implicit criteria made as explicit as possible, and if the formal communication system will not do the job, he must look elsewhere.

COMMITTEES

Of all the areas in which academics can waste time, the committee is probably the most famous, and deservedly so. (However, the time actually wasted is usually doubled by the time spent in complaining about how much time is wasted on committees.) There are usually at least two levels of committee status: the "major league" committees such as the senate and executive committees that appear to have some role in the formulation and implementation of academic policy and programs and the "minor league" ones (often with students as members) in such areas as landscaping, selecting the homecoming queen, and composing new food-service menus. Clearly, an infinite number of minor league committees are possible on any campus. The new instructor most likely will be on a minor, not a major, committee. Additionally, he has the problem of not knowing which committee to go to when he wants some action taken on his behalf. On both problems, the following list of questions might be useful.

Who are the committee members supposed to represent—themselves, or a larger body?

Does this committee establish, revise, review, or implement policy? Or does it recommend policies to other groups?

Are the responsibilities of the committee written down?

How often does the committee meet? Why?

Who votes?

How does one get on the committee? Who selects the chairman?

How is the agenda established?

To whom do the committee's decisions go? For what type of action?

What has the committee accomplished in the past two or three years?

Committee service is often one criterion for promotion, but this is usually interpreted as meaning willingness to serve on committees rather than a total dedication. To be crass, if one avoids committee work, it might be held against him, but if one becomes fiercely dedicated to committee work, it may not be a mark in his favor. (Indeed, few if any institutions have ratings of quality of faculty committee participation!) One should probably undertake a first committee assignment with good humor, seeing the task as a good source of information about the institution and as a way of tapping into communication, if not decision-making, networks. One problem to avoid is the chairmen's temptation to load up the new committee member with clerical busywork. By being overly eager to serve, the new faculty member can find himself so loaded down with minor departmental and committee tasks that his teaching and other major responsibilities suffer. When this happens, one should call a halt to further committee burdens as gracefully as possible.

Some committees find that their activities are largely for the purpose of justifying the existence of the committee. To find out whether or not to present a problem to a given committee, a young teacher might be wise to determine the "flow" of the committee by finding a previous matter similar to the one he is concerned with and finding out how the committee responded to it and what the outcome was. It may be that someone in the administration can get action faster than the committee. This is not necessarily "going around end," as most committee responsibilities are rather loosely defined, and if one is out of line, the administrator will usually send him to the proper place for the request or proposal. Department chairmen can also serve in this role. For such matters as the approval of a new course, the department chairman in some places can handle the matter virtually by himself; in other places the process of getting a new course approved is incredibly tedious and may take an entire year and cause some hard feelings. It might be well to test the wind on this issue before attempting to revolutionize the entire curriculum in the first year. Curriculum change is often the slowest type of change; a rule of thumb is that it takes about five times as long to change the curriculum as it does to fire the football coach.

It is sad, but true, that in American society there are something like 5,000 laws that are on the books but have never been enforced. Similarly, when the new faculty member looks at the mass of rules and regulations he must abide by, he tends to forget that the same thing is generally true with colleges and universities—if one obeyed *all* the rules he would never get anything done. There is some give in all social systems, and just as some students quickly learn that Professor Smith does not grade down for late papers (and thus gets most of his papers after the deadline), so some registrars insist that all instructors must have their grades in by December 23, yet faculty grades come in weeks later. It is a good idea not to experiment with one's own future by handing grades in late, but one can easily find out what rules and responsibilities *are* important. Again, one easy way to find out how things work is to follow a typical event as one would follow a stick of wood floating down a curving stream. Considering our simile, try ordering some sticks of wood called pencils. If it can be done in an unobtrusive way, trace the various stages the order follows through the recording and distribution systems. Compare, then, the way most experienced faculty get pencils to the way they are supposed to get them, and you will have a good idea of the limits of the selective-negligence system. It generally operates in some of the following: (1) taking of attendance and reporting of absences, (2) ordering of supplies, (3) increasing or decreasing of class size, (4) formulating of criteria for determining a "full load," (5) number of hours to be spent weekly with advisees, (6) reporting of all changes in class location and time of meeting, and (7) number of examinations and papers required.

One should not assume, however, that any area actually functions on the selective-negligence principle. One should first ascertain what colleagues do, in as unobtrusive a way as possible. Perhaps the greatest problem faced by the new teacher, in terms of selective negligence, is in the classroom itself, in the introductory or survey course. His training has pointed him to the virtues of specialized knowledge, and now he finds himself in charge, not of a seminar on Thomas Wentworth Higginson and the Secret Six, but of Introduction to American History, Leif Ericson to the Present. By definition, he must neglect much of the specialized knowledge he has acquired in one small compartment of this area and must try to cover the whole thing. In departments in which there is a common syllabus for these introductory courses, the problem is not so great. But where the teacher is on his own, he would do well to remember what he was like when he took his first course in the area. Instead of seeing the survey course as an insult to his duty to specialization, he might turn the problem around, asking: What material is really important enough to be worth including?

THE NEW FACULTY MEMBER AND ACTIVISM

Depending on the campus, considerable pressure may be brought to bear on the new faculty member to join in various protests, active or passive, against campus, state, or national policies. This pressure may come from students, outsiders, and faculty colleagues. The issues may range from the Vietnam war to liberalized student social regulations to a strike for higher salaries. Participation in such matters is, of course, a matter for individual conscience, after a careful investigation of the issues. But one should be aware of who one's allies are, what the consequences of participation are likely to be, and what the chances are for success. This is important, as students have been known to play one faculty member or faction off against another and even to con them into participating. Administrators, on the other hand, can be very convincing on the virtues of nonparticipation. The new instructor is vulnerable to student appeals for participation, as he is teaching-oriented and wants to be liked and respected, particularly as a man who "has a conscience," by his students. But student movements fluctuate with great speed, and the students who lead them fluctuate from place to place with even greater speed. If one does get involved, it is wise to be reasonably certain that one's allies will be around long enough to see the matter through. It is easier for a protesting student to get into another college than it is for the new instructor to get another position.

Some of these principles apply to intrafaculty matters as well. If a faculty member is attempting to develop a following in order to completely revise the policies and structures of the faculty and administration, it would be well to make sure that that gentleman is not planning to leave for another position the following year. It is wise to get involved with people who plan to stay and see the work through, whether it be an ad hoc committee, a professional association, a labor union, or whatever. Before joining any organization that is against the established order, a wise person, rather than accepting someone else's word, makes sure for himself that the established order is incapable of dealing with the given problem. To remain as independent and rational as possible in these pressure-filled situations is to act in the best traditions of academic freedom. The demagogue has no place in a professional faculty.

The thesis of this paper is that full participation of new faculty in the affairs of the campus should not be delayed until three years of service have been acquired. (In most situations about 3 or 4 *days* of careful looking and listening will provide enough information for meaningful participation.) It is not that new faculty do not push the levers, the problem is that they often push the wrong ones. It is almost impossible to generalize on what the right ones are, but the pitfalls that have been discussed here have a certain universal quality. Perhaps the most important quality in governance is mental set. If the new faculty member were to say on the way to work each morning, "The entire structure of this campus is deployed for only one reason—to assist *me* in the all-important work I alone can do in teaching students," a self-fulfilling prophecy might be created and the campus might begin to work in this way. If it did, everyone would certainly be better off.

Bibliography

American Association for Higher Education. *Decision Making in Higher Education.* Papers from the summer conference, 1968. Washington: American Association for Higher Education, 1968.

Caffrey, John. *The Future Academic Community: Continuity and Change.* Washington: American Council on Education, 1969.

Foote, Caleb, et al. *The Culture of the University: Governance and Education.* San Francisco: Jossey-Bass, 1968.

Hodgkinson, Harold. "Governance and Factions: Who Decides Who Decides?" Center for Research and Development in Higher Education, University of California, Berkeley, *Research Reporter* 3, no. 1 (1968).

———. "Students and an Intellectual Community." *Educational Record,* fall 1968, pp. 398-406.

Singletary, Otis A. *Freedom and Order on the Campus.* Washington: American Council on Education, 1968.

Temple Plan for University Governance, The. Philadelphia: Temple University, 1968.

Weber, Arnold, et al. *Faculty Participation in Academic Governance.* Washington: American Association for Higher Education, 1967.

Bibliographies
for Additional Fields

As stated in the preface, this volume is a selection of chapters from a full report submitted to the U. S. Office of Education. The bibliographies from the chapters included in that report but not included in this volume are below.

WALLACE W. DOUGLAS   LITERATURE

Cox, Harvey. "Underground Churches, Underground Schools." *Commonweal,* 13 December 1968, pp. 376-78.

Crane, Ronald S. "Questions and Answers in the Teaching of Literary Texts." In *The Idea of the Humanities and Other Essays Critical and Historical.* 2 vols. Chicago: University of Chicago Press, 1967.

Featherstone, Joseph. "Experiments in Learning." *The New Republic,* 14 December 1968, pp. 23-25.

Palmer, J. H. *The Rise of English Studies.* New York: Oxford University Press, 1965.

Parker, William Riley. "The Future of the 'Modern Humanities.'" Address to the Jubilee Congress of the Modern Humanities Research Association, August 1968, Cambridge University. Mimeographed in Indiana University English Department "Newsletter," 2 December 1968, pp. 69-81.

————. "Where Do English Departments Come From?" *College English* 28 (1967): 339-51.

JAMES M. McCRIMMON   VERBAL COMMUNICATION

The following selective list of books deals with various aspects of verbal communication. Since most of the items cited contain bibliographies of their own, this list may be used as a starting point for further investigation. In addition, the leading journals dealing with communication are excellent sources for articles: *College English, College Composition and Communication, The Quarterly Journal of Speech,* and the *Harvard Educational Review.*

Baugh, Albert C. *A History of the English Language.* New York: Appleton-Century-Crofts, 1957.
    The standard history.

Berlo, David K. *The Process of Communication.* New York: Holt, Rinehart & Winston, 1960.
    A good college textbook on verbal communication.

Brooks, Cleanth, and Warren, R. P. *Modern Rhetoric.* 2nd ed. New York: Harcourt, Brace & World, 1958.
    One of the major college textbooks on composition.

Chomsky, Noam. *Aspects of the Theory of Syntax.* Cambridge, Mass.: M.I.T. Press, 1965.
    The bible of transformational grammar, but because of its difficulty some readers will prefer to start with a simpler treatment, such as that of Thomas below.

Corbett, Edward P. J. *Classical Rhetoric for the Modern Student.* New York: Oxford University Press, 1965.
The best application of classical rhetoric to college composition.

Corbin, Richard, et al., eds. *Language Programs For the Disadvantaged.* Champaign, Ill.: National Council of Teachers of English, 1965.
Report of an NCTE committee on the teaching of English to the disadvantaged. Although chiefly concerned with elementary and secondary schools, the work offers a helpful analysis of a problem that is becoming common in colleges.

Francis, W. Nelson. *The Structure of American English.* New York: Ronald Press, 1958.
A good example of the structural approach to linguistics.

Gorrell, Robert M., ed. *Rhetoric: Theories for Application.* Champaign, Ill.: National Council of Teachers of English, 1967.
An anthology of articles dealing with the new rhetorics. This volume supplements that of Steinmann below.

Guth, Hans P. *English Today and Tomorrow.* Englewood Cliffs, N.J.: Prentice-Hall, 1964.
A comprehensive guide for teachers of English.

Hayakawa, S. I. *Language in Thought and Action.* 2nd ed. New York: Harcourt, Brace & World, 1964.
A popularization of Alfred Korzybski's *Science and Sanity* and the most readable introduction to semantics.

Kitzhaber, Albert R. *Themes, Theories, and Therapy: The Teaching of Writing in College.* New York: McGraw-Hill Book Co., 1963.
An authoritative criticism of the freshman-composition course.

Koestler, Arthur. *The Act of Creation.* New York: Macmillan Co., 1964.
Also available in paperback. A study of the conscious and unconscious processes in humor, scientific discovery, and art. A major contribution to the study of invention.

McCrimmon, James M. *Writing with a Purpose.* 4th ed. Boston: Houghton Mifflin Co., 1967.
A composition textbook influenced by the new rhetorics. The first two chapters deal in detail with prewriting.

Moffett, James. *Teaching the Universe of Discourse.* Boston: Houghton Mifflin Co., 1968.
Presents a rationale for a language-arts curriculum in elementary and secondary schools. Useful to the college teacher for its criticism of existing curricula.

Ogden, C. K., and Richards, I. A. *The Meaning of Meaning.* 8th ed. New York: Harcourt, Brace & World, 1946.
Also available as Harvest Book paperback. One of the earliest and most influential works on semantics.

Richards, I. A. *How to Read a Page.* New York: W. W. Norton & Co., 1942.
Written in reply to a popular book on reading. Richards's thesis is that reading is a difficult art and the best way to practice it is to be aware of the "great" words that cause most of the trouble.

———. *The Philosophy of Rhetoric.* New York: Oxford University Press, 1936.
Also available in paperback. A series of lectures emphasizing the need for a new rhetoric that is primarily concerned with removing the misunderstandings caused by our uses of language.

Saporta, Sol. *Psycholinguistics: A Book of Readings.* New York: Holt, Rinehart & Winston, 1961.
An anthology showing the interdisciplinary nature of modern scholarship in language.

Steinmann, Martin, Jr., ed. *New Rhetorics.* New York: Charles Scribner's Sons, 1967.
An anthology of articles on the new rhetorics.

Thomas, Owen. *Transformational Grammar and the Teaching of English.* New York: Holt, Rinehart & Winston, 1965.
A simplified account of transformational grammar.

Windes, Russell R., ed. *The Bobbs-Merrill Series in Speech Communication.* Indianapolis, Ind.: Bobbs-Merrill Co., 1966.
A series of twelve small paperback volumes, each of which deals with a separate phase of oral communication—for example, audience analysis, message preparation, ethics of speech communication, communication behavior.

SHELDON JUDSON   EARTH SCIENCES

Hutton, James. *Theory of the Earth.* 1795.

Judson, Sheldon. "Geomorphology and Geology." *Transactions of the New York Academy of Sciences,* 2nd ser., vol. 20, no. 4(1958): 305-15.

Knopf, Adolf. "The Geologic Records of Time." In *Time and Its Mysteries,* 3rd series. New York: New York University Press, 1949.

W. T. LIPPINCOTT   CHEMISTRY

College-chemistry teaching

Hutchinson, Eric. "Fashion in Science and in the Teaching of Science." *Journal of Chemical Education* 45 (1968): 600.

———. "Science, A Component of Liberal Education." *Journal of Chemical Education* 44 (1967): 261.

Weinberg, Alvin M. "The Two Faces of Science." *Journal of Chemical Education* 45 (1968): 74.

Elaboration on the subject

Handbook for Chemistry Assistants. Easton, Pa.: Chemical Education Publishing Co., 1967.

Woodburn, John H., and Obourn, Ellsworth S. *Teaching in the Pursuit of Science.* New York: Macmillan Co., 1965.

Young, J. A. "What Should Students Do in the Laboratory?" *Journal of Chemical Education* 45 (1968): 798.

Detailed information on hardware and software of innovation

Barnard, W. R. "Teaching Aids." *Journal of Chemical Education* 45 (1968): 63, 136, 206, 341, 543, 617, 681, 745.

Modern Teaching Aids for College Chemistry. Advisory Council on College Chemistry serial publication no. 18, 1966.

Additional reading on content and curriculum

"Recent Trends in Undergraduate Chemistry Curricula." *Journal of Chemical Education* 41 (1964): 126-47.

"Symposium on Chemistry for Non-Science Majors." *Journal of Chemical Education* 45 (1968): 550; 46 (1969): 64, 66, 69.

LEONARD J. FEIN   POLITICAL SCIENCE

Somit, Albert, and Tanenhaus, Joseph. *American Political Science*. New York: Atherton Press, 1964.

HENRY CORD MEYER   HISTORY

Portions of the following books will be of interest to young historian-teachers.

Association of American Colleges. *Non-Western Studies in the Liberal Arts College*. Washington, D.C.: American Council on Education, 1964.

Cantor, Norman E., and Schneider, Richard I. *How to Study History*. New York: T. Y. Crowell, 1967.

Carpenter, Peter. *History Teaching: The Era Approach*. New York: Cambridge University Press, 1964.

Elton, G. R. *The Practice of History*. New York: T. Y. Crowell, 1967.

François, Michel, et al. *Historical Study in the West*. . . . Introduction by Boyd C. Shafer. New York: Appleton-Century-Crofts, 1968.

Gustavson, Carl G. *A Preface to History*. New York: McGraw-Hill Book Co., 1955.

Hughes, H. Stuart. *History as Art and as Science*. New York: Harper & Row, 1964.

Roucek, Joseph S., ed. *The Teaching of History*. New York: Philosophical Library, 1967.

Smith, Page. *The Historian and History*. New York: Alfred A. Knopf, 1964.

Ward, Paul L. *A Style of History for Beginners*. Washington: American Historical Society, 1959.

Some pertinent articles

Bailey, Jackson H. "Non-Western Studies in the Small Liberal Arts College . . . " *Liberal Education* 47 (1961): 405-11.

Cohen, Maurice. "Toward a Basic Undergraduate Course in World Civilization." *Liberal Education* 51 (1965): 209-20.

Finkelstein, Joseph. "Freshman History: The Neglected Course." *Liberal Education* 46 (1960): 267-72.

Geiger, Louis S. "Recruiting History Faculty: The Liberal Arts College." *Liberal Education* 54 (1968): 294-99.

Keeney, Barnaby C. "The Dilemmas of Relevance and Commitment." *Liberal Education* 52 (1966): 27-33.

Means, Richard L. "Research vs. Teaching: Is There a Genuine Conflict?" *Liberal Education* 54 (1968): 238-44.

Paige, Glen D. "The Professor and Politics." *AAUP Bulletin* 52 (1966): 52-56.

Perkins, Dexter. "We Shall Gladly Teach." *American Historical Review* 62 (1956-57): 291-309.

Shafer, Boyd C. "The Study of History in the United States." *AAUP Bulletin* 50 (1964): 232-40.